HOPE FOR
FREEDOM

DANA EPPERLY

Hope For Freedom
My Journey Out of Emotional Addiction & the Lesbian Lifestyle

ISBN: 978-0-9986849-4-9 (Print)
ISBN: 978-0-9986849-5-6 (e-book)

Editor: Charity Bradshaw
www.charitybradshaw.com

Publisher: LifeWise Books
PO BOX 1072
Pinehurst, TX 77362
www.lifewisebooks.com

Printed in the USA

Endorsements

"Rarely does one bare their heart as Dana has to reveal the intense tug-of-war over her soul and the journey to find her true identity. This books shows how God never lets us go."

Rhonda Hostetter
Founder of INSPIRE Business Community

"Readers, whether your struggle is with a lesbian lifestyle or any other kind of "war of the soul", you will find in Dana a compassionate and encouraging trench-mate. She understands addiction and being wounded from a deep-down honest place in her heart, and she has fought a tremendous battle to become free and vibrant and real.

Dana decided that "crumbs and scraps" were not what she was created for. She describes in vivid detail the "fight to get to Jesus." Although the intense pain that she went through for many months was not understandable to her at the time, she has come to accept that it was the "loving discipline" of the Lord, which brought about the Great Exchange: trading in her desperate sense of rejection and brokenness for the Master Weaver's acceptance and love, freedom and wholeness."

Susan M Austin MD
Inward-bound-adventures.net

Dana invites us into the slow but steep descent of a woman believing her best and maybe only option was another woman. She does so without self-pity and without demonizing anyone. I have not read a story that combines such realism with genuine affection and honor for loving, flawed family members. Most importantly, Dana conveys the tenacious, ever ascending love of God that met her over and over again until she found her footing and a clear path for freedom.

Andrew Comiskey
Executive Director
Desert Stream Ministries

Dedication

This book is dedicated to my Mom and Dad.

Thank you for never giving up on me. Words could never express the deep gratitude that is in my heart. It is through your love and encouragement that I made it to the other side.

Acknowledgments

First and foremost, I want to thank my **Lord Jesus Christ** for the sweetness of your tender love, your long suffering, and for never giving up on me. Thank you for your faithfulness in seeing me through until I was safe in your loving arms. I love you.

To my **Mom and Dad**: for being tenacious warriors for God's Kingdom. It is through your tenacious faith that I am walking in freedom today. Thank you for walking through it with me and believing in me.

Mom, for all the years and tears of long-suffering for me, thank you.

Dad, for all the silent tears you wept for me and for your long-suffering for me, thank you.

Your love and faith in God's providence has strengthened me to the core of my soul. Your love has anchored me in God's truth and pulled me up to see the light of Jesus.

I am eternally grateful for you both. I know God has a special crown waiting for you on the other side of Heaven. I encourage you both to finish this race strong. I encourage you to go for the gold, holding nothing back. I love you.

To my precious sister **Lis**, who has walked alongside me through my writing process. Thank you for your joyous work helping me birth this book. I will never forget the grace and patience you showed me. Thank you for all the hours of editing and for putting up with me. You're a real trooper! Most of all, thank you for your friendship and for believing in me. You reflect the love of Christ by being a faithful friend to me. (Proverbs 17:17) I love you.

To my beautiful sister, **Melanie**, thank you for being a solid rock for me on this journey. We have been through it all together. Thank you for your gentle encouragement and strength that comes from your trust in the Lord. Thank you for saying, "yes" to God, and for your faithfulness to Him. It has strengthened my faith more than you know.

Thank you for standing on the truth of God's word and never settling for compromise. You are a mighty warrior for God who pushes back the darkness every day. Thank you for your courage and bravery. (Joshua 1:7-9) You are a brave soul. I am so proud of you. I love you.

To my little brother, **Chad** (Nae), Thank you for loving me through it all. You always see my heart and love me unconditionally. Thank you for never judging me and for loving me well in spite of all my weaknesses. We have always had a special closeness and your love is precious to me. I honor and treasure you for the loving man and father you have become.

Chad, there's gold in you and your heart is full of love. I pray you will see what I see when I look at you and that one day you might be able to comprehend how great God's love is for you. (Ephesians 3:18) I love you.

To my precious **Page**...when God gave you to my brother in marriage, He blessed me with another sister. Thank you for being such a good listener throughout my journey and for believing in me. You are a beautiful reflection of Jesus and have always modeled the tender love of Christ. I treasure you as a sister and friend. Thank you for being a beautiful mother to my nephews. I love you.

To my fun- loving nephews...

Connor Eric... for your fiery yet sweet spirit. You will set the world on fire with your tenacious spirit! I love you.

Colin Edward...for your audacious but gentle spirit. You will draw all men to Jesus' tender love. I love you.

Case Easton...for your smile that lights up a room. You will shine like the sun and be a blazing light in the world. I love you.

To my sweet friend, **Tammy Caffey**, thank you for your love and support throughout this writing process. Thank you for taking the initiative in helping me launch my book with your creative ideas. I never asked you for help yet you generously volunteered without hesitation. Thank you for all you do in building the Kingdom of God. Your generosity and kindness will never be forgotten. I love you.

To all of my family, friends and prayer warriors who have covered me and contended for me in this season of writing, I couldn't have done it without you. Thank you so much. I love you.

To **Desert Stream Ministries**, thank you for being a healing place for the sexually and relationally broken. You are salt and light to the Body of Christ. Thank you for all your work to help people walk in freedom and wholeness. Your ministry has truly helped me see that I am a good gift to the Body of Christ.

Last but not least, I would like to thank every priest, pastor and servant of the Lord that has come alongside me in my journey of sexual healing and wholeness. Your love has challenged me to have an authentic love for the Body of Christ.

Contents

The thief comes only to steal

and kill and destroy.

I came that they may have life

and have it abundantly.

John 10:10 (ESV)

1

THE EARLY YEARS

"Grandpa, Tell me 'bout the good old days.
Sometimes it feels like this world's gone crazy.
Grandpa, take me back to yesterday,
Where the line between right and wrong
Didn't seem so hazy." [1]
-The Judds

Solid Foundation

One of my earliest memories is of my daddy twirling me around and carrying me on his shoulders outside of our little white trailer house where I grew up in Southeast Texas. It was around 1975, and I remember the sun was shining bright outside as was the light inside my heart. Love and joy filled my little, tender heart. I remember feeling so safe with him. He would hold tight to my tiny legs while spinning me around and around on his shoulders. He loved rough-housing and playing with me when I was a little girl.

When Daddy would put me on his shoulders, I felt like I was so special and perfect. I felt like a princess...like I was perfect in his eyes. I remember his eyes would dance and sparkle when he smiled at me. His love and strength were constant to me while I was growing up. He took me everywhere with him. I remember standing right up under his arm as close as I could to him while he was driving. He owned a green 1970 Roadrunner sports car. As long as I was close to Daddy, everything was going to be ok. I naturally developed a strong foundation of love and trust with him.

As a little one, I remember my Momma being sweet-spirited and super protective. She loved me more than life itself, all the way to the moon and back. Her love was steadfast and she was so proud of me. I felt like I was her little princess, her "precious one." I was twenty-months old when I vividly remember momma telling me about "my baby sister." She led me through the long hallway into the back room where my baby sister was lying in a crib. I climbed up and up to the top (with her help) until I finally laid my eyes on the most beautiful face I had ever seen. I repeatedly said, "baby?" as if I was asking if she was mine. I thought she was my gift from them. I literally thought she was mine. I fell in love with my sister, Melanie, from the moment I met her. Melanie was my constant companion and a sheer joy from that moment on. Although opposites, we were inseparable like two peas in a pod.

As children, Melanie and I spent every waking moment together. We would wake up early every Saturday morning and watch cartoons from 6:30am until we were ready to hit the trails. We couldn't wait to go to the woods across the street and make our own "secret trails." It was our thing. We had a routine before we would go out and play in the woods across the street. Melanie would go to Dad's work shed in the backyard and get her bb gun and Dad's machete. I would pack us a lunch and snacks for our adventures. We made a great team!

Melanie would clear cut all the sticker bushes and small trees while I would follow her making the way clearer and smoother using sticks. In spite of the hot, South Texas summers, nothing would stop us from going out to the woods, making new trails and riding our "Big Red" three-wheeler. We spent many days in those woods from sun up to sun down. It was always refreshing to hear Momma calling us to come home in the evenings (although we would ignore her call if we were not ready to come home) because supper was ready. Momma always prepared a delicious supper for us which almost always included rice and gravy…still one of my favorite southern foods.

When I was about six, I remember Momma singing old country songs to Melanie and me. One of her favorite country songs was "Don't it make your brown eyes blue." Every time that song would come on the radio she would sing along with Crystal Gayle to Melanie and me. Melanie had piercing blue eyes and I had big brown eyes. When Momma would sing that song to us she would point to my sister for the blue-eyed part and then she would point to me for the brown-eyed part. It would always make me feel that I was unique and special. She enjoyed singing country songs to us while swinging together on our wooden swing on the back patio.

One day, my Dad brought home a used 150 racing motorcycle. He forbid us to ride it while he was working. Finally, Dad showed us how to crank that bad boy up. He showed us how to use a mop bucket to climb on since we were too short to get on the bike on our own. We already knew how to shift the gears from our time on our three-wheeler. A couple of days later, Dad was working on a hot, summer day. Melanie and I were bored and we couldn't stop thinking about that motorcycle sitting in the shed.

Melanie said, "Dana, you want to take that motorcycle out for a little spin?"

I was reluctant to answer because I knew Dad told us not to take it out when he wasn't there. It was a big bike for us young girls, and powerful too. We were probably around nine and ten years old.

Melanie insisted that we test drive it so we scoped it out. We couldn't let Momma see or hear what we were doing so we quickly snuck in the house and tried to locate her. We didn't see her so we hurried out to the shed in the back and did everything Dad told us to do to get it started. When we finally got it fired up, it was so loud. It seemed even louder because we were trying to sneak around. I thought for sure Mom was going to hear that roar and seal our disciplinary fate. In order to avoid that premature intervention, we jumped on it using the mop bucket as a stool in a hurry.

Of course, I let Melanie drive. She always wanted to lead. What a big mistake. We took off down our street with the engine wide open. As we got about halfway down the road we were flying. I gripped tightly to Melanie's little waist, and I looked over her shoulders to see the odometer. I knew we were going way too fast. We were pushing nearly 80 miles per hour.

At that moment, we were quickly approaching the end of our road and I just knew we were going to wreck. There was no possible way Melanie would be able to stop soon enough to avoid a crash. I screamed out franticly, "Slow down Melanie!"

As we began taking the corner, the bike was almost touching the ground and we were still going extremely fast. I will never forget the feeling I had at that moment. We should have crashed and burned but something miraculous happened. We went all the way down with that bike and something miraculously popped us back up.

I immediately told Melanie, "Take me back home."

I wanted off that motorcycle. I knew God was with us and had spared us that day. We never took the bike out again without Dad being home and never told him about this until years later.

Cajun Roots

My Momma is Cajun French, and was raised as a devout Catholic in a small town called Oberlin in South

Louisiana. Our family road trips to Louisiana were soothing to my soul. I remember climbing in the back seat of our family car (a long brown car) with my sister to make the lengthy trips. While traveling, Melanie always wanted to sleep on the floor board and I slept on the back seat of that long boat.

I always anticipated and treasured these trips and especially getting to visit our grandparents. It took a couple of hours to get there, which seemed like eternity for us kiddos. One of my favorite parts of our visits to Oberlin was soft serve ice-cream at the Frosty. The Frosty was a run-down, tiny shack that had a few groceries, lots of candy, and a pool hall in the back. I remember the smell of their homemade hamburgers coming out of the sliding glass window where we would place our order. We would all order a large vanilla ice cream in a cup.

Maw-maw and Paw-paw (Mom's parents) spoke in French often times when they didn't want us kids knowing what they were talking about. When we would stay the night in Oberlin, I remember Maw-Maw telling all of us children and adults to get on our knees. It was time to pray as a family. We would gather around the living room and pray the family rosary together before we would go to bed. It always brought such peace to me as a child.

As a young girl, I remember Momma telling us the intense story of when my Paw-Paw surrendered his life to Jesus. This story stayed close to my heart and made such an impact on me throughout my life. Momma told us that Paw-Paw was a good man who loved his family but was also an alcoholic when she and her four siblings were young. He would go to the bar down the road regularly and get slopping drunk. Some nights he was gone for hours at a time. Occasionally Maw-Maw would walk to the bars in the early morning hours to find him and someone to bring him home since they didn't own a vehicle.

I was told that Paw-Paw would feel so guilty after getting drunk, but he didn't know how to stop drinking. He was a binge drinker that couldn't manage to get control of himself. One day, he had just come off an all-night bender, and had to go feed the farm animals at his parents' house in the country since his parents were out of town. After feeding the animals, he stood in the living room where there was a picture of Jesus hanging on the wall. When he saw that picture, he fell on his knees and cried out to God. He felt that Jesus "came alive" to him while gazing at that picture. Paw-Paw encountered Jesus' love and mercy in such a powerful way that he never took another sip of alcohol after that moment.

My Dad was raised in a little farm town in Welsh, Louisiana about 30 miles south of Oberlin. He picked cotton and farmed in the fields as a young boy I remember my Mee-Maw always cooking and caring for children and her neighbors. She didn't have much to give but she gave of her time and love. Pee-Paw was a quiet and kind man who worked hard to make a living. Every time we would go for a visit he would hold Melanie and I on his knees and give us each a pack of gum. He usually gave us Wrigley's Big Red or Juicy Fruit gum. He was so proud of us. Mee-Maw was very playful and creative with us. She made up all sorts of games and even showed us how to catch mosquito hawks (without tearing their wings) on her clothes line in her backyard.

Some of my favorite memories were going to the railroad tracks down the road with my cousins from Laplace, Louisiana. We would each put a penny on the track and then wait and wait. Sometimes we would wait for hours for a train to come to flatten our pennies. It was okay though because it was our time to dream, laugh, and share our childhood stories with one another. I loved spending the night there, too. They didn't have central air back then, but they did have this enormous window fan that made a welcomed and calming noise. I loved falling asleep to that sound.

Dad was raised in the Methodist church but didn't attend church as an adult. He wanted to join Momma, Melanie and me so that we could go to church as a family. He began meeting with Father Pat, Mom's parish priest at the time. Shortly thereafter, my dad was so affected by the love Father Pat represented that he converted to Catholicism.

Childlike Faith

When I was a little girl, I felt a deep love for Jesus. As far back as I can remember, I had a strong sense and awareness of God. I had a tender heart and I loved people. I could often feel people's pain in my heart. As far back as I can remember, I could see into the depths of people's hearts. I had a keen sense of discernment of what was right and wrong at an early age. I sensed God's presence deeply and all the while experienced the darkness as well.

As a little girl, I remember looking through our big family Bible that sat on our brown coffee table. It must have weighed more than I did. I liked it especially because it had pictures in it. I can remember Mom reading us the picture captions that were in there. Out of all the Bible stories and pictures, it was the picture of Jesus's death on a cross that really drew me. It didn't scare me. It captivated me! I deeply desired to know about that man.

As a Roman Catholic, I went to weekly classes to learn about Jesus, study the word of God, and prepare for all the sacraments. I was 7 years old when I started preparing to receive Jesus in Holy Communion. I remember my first communion teacher, Mrs. Mires. She was a humble, kind and loving lady. Her eyes sparkled when she talked about Jesus. She talked about Him as if she really knew Him. She taught me how important it was to be prepared in my heart to receive Jesus in my first Holy Communion.

Mrs. Mires emphasized the importance of knowing that it was truly Jesus that we would receive in communion.

"I want to tell you that this is a special time when Jesus will come in to your hearts in a real way. He wants to come and live in your hearts." she said.

Although I didn't understand it in my mind, I believed it in my heart. I couldn't wait until the day I could receive

Jesus in Holy Communion! It was like I was waiting to unwrap my biggest Christmas present of all times.

Finally, the day arrived. Family and friends gathered for this joyous celebration. Momma dressed me in a beautiful white dress, with white lacy socks and white dress sandals. I felt beautiful, special, and so loved. I wore a beautiful white sash that draped over me with my name on it in big, red, bold letters—DANA. It was special to see my name written on it. I felt like God knew me by my name. I believed that Jesus was waiting for me at the altar.

I was nervous as I slowly walked up the long aisle to get to the altar. The priest looked into my eyes and held the host up high.

"The Body of Christ.", he said.

"Amen." I answered.

When I received Holy Communion, I remember feeling overwhelmed by Jesus' tender love that flooded my heart. Jesus was real and present inside me. I felt His love for me. I felt so pure. I experienced His love and peace. It was so joyful.

Surprise!

One morning, when I was about ten years old, I stayed home from school because I was sick. Apparently, Mom had been feeling under the weather too. I remember Dad driving us to the doctor. Dad and I were sitting in the car waiting on Mom to come out of the doctor's office. When she finally came out, she was smiling.

She looked at us grinning from ear to ear and said, "I'm pregnant."

I was shocked.

"You're making that up," Dad said in disbelief.

"Honey, I'm pregnant! You want me to go and get Carol?" Mom said.

Carol was our family nurse.

"Yes." he said. Dad needed proof!

A few minutes later, Carol came back outside with mom and both of them were smiling.

Carol looked at my Dad and said, "You're going to have another little Epperly."

It was surprising to all of us since Mom had a difficult time getting pregnant with my sister and me. She had to take fertility medication to get pregnant with us. The doctor had informed my mom that she probably wouldn't be able to have any more kids.

Months and months went by. It seemed like an eternity waiting on our new addition to the family! Melanie and I were so anxious for Mom to have the baby. I had just turned eleven the month before she delivered on September 4, 1984. Melanie and I rode the school bus home that day and Aunt Janet was waiting in the driveway for us.

"Your Momma is having the baby!" she said.

I couldn't wait to find out if it was a little sister or brother. Back in those days you couldn't find out ahead of time what the sex of the baby was. You just had to wait.

We gathered all our stuff for the night and went to my Aunt Janet's house a few blocks away. Dad finally showed up that evening and told us it was a boy! I remember dad walking Melanie and I up to the nursery. We diligently looked and looked through the somewhat foggy glass of the nursery. Dad, being the jokester he is, pretended like he didn't know where our brother Chad was in the nursery. He made us guess several times. Finally, I saw my baby brother for the first time through the glass. He was the most beautiful baby I had ever seen.

A few days passed, and Melanie and I got off of the school bus and discovered that Mom and Chad were home. We ran to the back room and were finally able to touch him. I held him in my arms for the first time in Dad's big red recliner in our living room. Chad was so perfect. He smelled so new. I fell in love with him the first time I held him in my arms.

It was a big adjustment in our family especially for Melanie and me since we were used to getting all the attention. Needless to say, Chad was always held and never lacked attention. Melanie and I would fight over him most of the time. The only time Melanie was willing to share was when Chad had a stinky diaper.

I remember Chad bringing so much joy in to our family. Our beloved Paw-Paw lived with us for two years before he passed away. Mom became pregnant with Chad two months after Paw-Paw passed. After losing him, Chad brought a new hope and new life into our family. He opened our hearts up again which was something I already needed because of some unfortunate circumstances that had happened a few years prior.

Innocence Lost

Before Chad was born, I had a friend from grade school that I would go and visit on occasional weekends. Her name was Ashley and she had two older brothers. Ashley and I were about eight years old at the time. Her brothers were teenagers, both around sixteen years old. One summer weekend we went out on their boat with her family to go skiing and joy riding. It was a blast to be out on the Cow Bayou playing on the water in the hot southeast Texas summer. All of us would take turns hydro sliding and skiing. Some of us would stay on the bank waiting for them to get back.

On one occasion, I was left with one of her brothers on the bank while everyone else was riding on the boat. The details are a little blurry as I have unwillingly blocked some of it out. I remember Ashley's brother, Kyle, trying to touch me in a sexual way. He made sexual gestures and told me what he would like to do to me sexually. When I went home that night, I vividly remember running to the bathroom to shower immediately. I felt like I couldn't get clean enough. I felt so dirty. I never told anyone what happened to me. That is all I remember.

On another occasion, I have a memory of a neighbor, Mary, who I visited on a regular basis. Mary and her brothers would come over to our house as well. We would all play together. There was a boy my age who on one occasion touched me sexually and violated me. I remember it feeling so wrong. I was paralyzed in fear when he touched me because I was so scared. I don't remember how many times it happened. I just remember dreading those games and avoiding being alone with him. I never told anyone because I felt guilty and shameful. I knew that I should have told him to stop touching me like that but I was extremely passive and shy on top of being terrified. This made me feel more shameful. The culmination of these traumatic events left me believing that boys were no longer safe. I stopped trusting and put up a huge barrier to guard my heart.

— 2 —

What is Wrong with Me?

Roots of Rejection

My family went to church together every Sunday morning. As far as I can remember, we never missed church unless someone was deathly ill. Growing up, I remember Dad worked hard to provide for us. He had a job with Texaco, a refinery. He worked shift work which consisted of both nights and days. He sacrificed for us to have good things. When he did something, he always gave 110%. He could build, fix, or rig anything that he put his hands on. There wasn't anything he couldn't do. "Can't" was not in his vocabulary and boy, was he head-strong and stubborn.

My dad was the strong protective father, but emotionally distant from me. Although he wanted to express his heart, he had a wall up and didn't allow people to break through. I often walked on eggshells trying to please him because he would get angry easily. In my little world, I tried to keep this distorted sense of peace within my family. I tried to please everyone and keep my family in harmony with each other.

As a child, I felt a heavy responsibility to keep the peace and be stable. I didn't dare rock the boat. Dad served as a US Marine in the Vietnam War which resulted in post-traumatic stress disorder. This caused much of his behavior to be hard for me because I was tender-hearted and sensitive. I often interpreted his "toughness" and "hardness" as rejection and a forceful blow to my spirit. This was especially difficult because my main love language was and is affirmation and words of acknowledgement.

He never liked for me to cry even as a little girl. He thought only sissies cried. He constantly wanted to toughen me up for the world, and wanting to please him, I always strained to be the perfect daughter. It felt like I could never measure up to his expectations which set the rejection in even deeper.

Mom worked hard to provide and take good care for us as well. She always yearned and strived to be the "best" mother and wife. She was constantly cleaning, cooking and picking up after us. I always remember her preparing delicious meals for our family. She definitely spoiled us with her cooking. Mom was passionate in preparing her delicious southern Cajun food. The aroma of her authentic Cajun gumbo roux filled the whole house till the next day. Our sheets would even smell the roux till the next morning. Chicken and sausage gumbo is still one of my favorites.

Mom had a dominant and controlling personality. If you didn't do it her way she would go behind your work and redo it whether it was sweeping the floor or making macaroni and cheese. My parents often butted heads because they were both young and stubborn. It caused a lot of friction and arguments within their marriage and our family.

My mom had specific expectations of how her daughters should look and act like and I definitely did not meet those. It felt like she always dreamed of me being a girly girl, wearing cute skirts and dresses. I didn't like wearing dresses largely because they weren't comfortable. Mom would often ask me why I didn't want to wear a dress, which made me feel like I wasn't girlie enough. It was like I was "less than" because I didn't conform to what girls were supposed to like. I thought something was wrong with me. I would ask myself, "Why am I so different?"

Because I was so shy, my mom would often speak for me and tell me what I liked, and what I didn't like. I was never allowed to have a voice for or opinion about what I really felt inside. It caused me to believe that my feelings didn't matter and even more, did *I* really matter? These feelings eventually closed my heart off from emotional connection, even though I deeply longed for it. I ended up feeling lost, insecure and unsure of myself with an ever-growing wall around my heart.

Emotional Starvation

In my grade school years, I developed a profound need and longing to be close to my girlfriends in school, especially on a deep emotional level. I just craved for someone to connect with me and my heart. At this point, boys seemed foreign, unsafe, and unfamiliar to me. Besides, I didn't trust them anyway.

I remember having sleep overs with my girlfriends in grade school. There were many nights I remember laying there, desiring to be noticed. I needed my voice to be heard, for someone to hear my heart. I wanted to be held so badly that I fantasized about my friends holding me tight. I craved approval, acceptance, and a deep longing for a true emotional connection. I just wanted to feel accepted and affirmed for being me. I didn't care what it looked like. I just had to have it. I was starving emotionally.

Diamond in the Rough?

Dad taught Melanie and I how to play softball when we were 4 and 5 years old. He worked with us on a regular basis teaching us how to hit the ball and to catch and throw the ball correctly. Dad put so much effort into teaching us so that we could be the best at whatever we did. We continued to play softball year after year. When Melanie and I were about 9 or 10 years old, Dad taught us how to pitch the softball. Melanie was a year younger than me so she was sometimes on a different team than I was.

After working with Melanie, Dad could see she had a knack for windmill fast pitching. She was amazing at it. I pitched as well, but I never could master the windmill. I also couldn't pitch as fast as Melanie could. I remember one specific day when Dad was working with us on pitching in the back yard. There was this moment when I noticed a distinct change in my heart. I remember this particular moment because it was when I realized all of Dad's attention had shifted to Melanie and her fast windmill pitching. I was left standing in the yard with my glove on. I remember feeling like I was completely pushed aside.

Logically, it made sense in my mind because Melanie was a better pitcher than me, but even still, a deep sense of rejection had taken root in my heart. I remember feeling like I wasn't good enough. I remember feeling passed over and second best. I felt like a diamond in the rough. Playing softball became a reminder to me of how I wasn't good enough. Melanie made All-Stars for softball almost every year and I never did. Each time it seemed to reiterate what I already felt. I wasn't good enough. I played softball every year until I was sixteen, all the while striving to "be good enough" only to feel like I never was.

I tried so hard to be liked, accepted, and to fit in with my peers in school. I desperately wanted to fit in somewhere. In junior high, I felt like I was the weirdo girl, the different one. I didn't like purses and therefore didn't carry one. There was never a good enough reason for me to lug a purse around school.

One of my classmates would harass me by saying, "You're weird, Dana. How come you don't carry a purse?"

The same girl would also harass me about not wearing make-up. She would glare at me as if I disgusted her. I had a mullet haircut in Junior High. That added to me not feeling like I fit in with the girls.

In seventh grade, one of my girl classmates asked me, "Dana, are you gay?"

As if I already didn't feel different and unaccepted enough. I didn't even know what "being gay" was. I was so sheltered, shy, and afraid; I would just sit there and take her verbal attacks and judgements. I didn't even defend or stand up for myself and no one else did either. I was afraid, never knew what to say, and was used to not having a voice anyway.

I remember dreading seventh grade basketball class. All of us girls changed in to our workout clothes in one big room inside the locker area. I was beyond shy and felt inadequate because all the girls were developed and I was not. I remember stressing out to rush through the hallway (sometimes run) to get to the locker room first so no one would see me naked while changing. I didn't want them to see how different I was or worse to point it out. It was so bad, that I found an old damp shower stall to change in. I hated the way this made me feel. I wanted to hide there the entire class or my whole life. It was always cold and clammy in there. It wasn't an ironclad escape because I could still hear some of the girls snickering and laughing at me for going in there to change.

I hated basketball. I wasn't any good at it. It required assertive physical contact. That wasn't me.

My coach would holler at me "Dana, be aggressive! Get in the game!"

It wasn't in me to be aggressive and push a girl down to get possession of the ball. I felt so out of place on the basketball court and in my life in general. Coach would frequently give me a look that said, "What's wrong with you?" I strived, but always fell short of what everyone wanted me to be. I hated the way that made me feel. I was trying to do and be something that I wasn't.

I didn't quite excel in academics throughout my school days either. I had terrible anxiety as a child and especially struggled the nights before tests. Studying for a test and concentrating in class were challenging as well. I didn't know it then, but looking back I think I had ADD growing up. I couldn't stay focused long enough to learn what I was studying. I remember Mom and Dad having to help me study for a test. We would go over the material for the test together then Mom or Dad would call out review questions. They would get so frustrated with me.

Mom would sometimes say to me, "What's wrong with you, Dana?"

Mom couldn't help but compare me to Melanie. She couldn't understand why it took me so much longer to grasp the material I was studying. I felt horrible about it and constantly strained to do better.

It left me with the same question of, "What is wrong with me?" I tried so hard to please everyone. I desperately wanted to be who everyone thought I should be. Yet all my efforts seemed like they were never noticed. Could anyone see me? My heart? My determination?

Proving Myself

I was determined to prove myself in some way so I could be accepted. This meant that I had to be especially good at something, right?! If I was really good at something, people would like me more, and maybe even notice me. There was only one problem, nothing really interested me or fired me up in school. I wanted to be noticed by the junior high guys, but it seemed that the ones I was interested in didn't have any interest in me. Most of my classmates had boyfriends, but no guy took interest in me. It left me with the same familiar feeling of, "What's wrong with me?" Since I struggled academically I had to prove myself somewhere else.

I decided to try volleyball. I didn't like it at first, but I became pretty good at it (which is funny because I am 5'1" on my tip toes). I learned quickly that spiking the ball wouldn't best suit my stature, so I worked hard and learned to be the best defensive player for my team. I made sure I was first place in all my training. I gave our practices all my heart and soon became the poster child for coming in first place in all our training whether it was suicides, arm crawls, or wall sits.

I was notorious for setting the bar high in our volleyball two-a-day trainings. My coach would call out all my teammates when she thought they were dragging too far behind me. I was finally getting some positive attention as a sophomore because of volleyball. My coach noticed me and my heart. She saw something in me.

I worked hard to get a starting position as a sophomore on the junior varsity volleyball team. I was also a setter and averaged 98% on all my saves per game. I was smokin'!

There was this one game we played away from home and I served 9-10 aces in a row to win the match and the game. My teammates were elated! They all picked me up together and held me up for our victory! I felt like a champion who was truly accepted and that I made a difference that day. I was noticed.

My junior year came around and again I worked hard to make varsity volleyball. I didn't make the varsity team but that was ok with me because I was just ecstatic about playing volleyball at all.

The first JV game began and coach didn't start me. I was ok that I didn't start, I'm sure Coach had her reasons and I could work with that. Time went on and I continued to sit on the bench waiting to go in. Before I realized it, the buzzer went off and the coach never put me in the game. Why? I was one of the best players and I deserved to play. The second game came, the third game came, and she would only put me in for a few minutes a game. It was barely long enough to touch the ball and maybe serve once. I was crushed. I didn't understand what had changed.

It didn't take long for me to start putting the puzzle pieces together. There was a new girl on my team whose parent was newly elected to the school board. The coach put her in my position. I was replaced. I wept over this situation. After all, I had earned my right to play. I was "good enough" to play.

Some of the other team parents saw me sitting on the bench and they would come to me and question me "Why aren't you playing, Dana?" They thought I was injured or something.

I didn't have an answer.

I asked Coach, "Why won't you play me?"

She never had an honest answer. "You have to prove it to me," she said.

From that day on, she never really gave me a chance. All I could think about was that I had already proven it the year before. It crushed my spirit. I had worked too hard to sit on the bench every game. The whole situation caused me to get physically sick and I developed an ulcer in my stomach from the anxiety. My dad went to the head coach and spoke with him about my situation. The head coach made promises that I would get to play but nothing changed.

Finally, I made the difficult decision to quit volleyball and concentrate solely on powerlifting. I felt like powerlifting was the best choice because it was an individual sport and no one could take my place away from me.

I had started lifting weights in the eighth grade. I had a God-given strength coupled with die-hard endurance. As a freshman, I had heard about a girl named Kristi, a senior cheerleader who both lifted and competed with the guys since there wasn't a girl's powerlifting team that was established yet. I thought to myself, I can do that. I want to do that.

My sophomore year, I finally convinced my best friend Tammy to go with me to ask the powerlifting and football coach, Coach Wilson, if we could try out for the girl's team. He was big in stature and rough around the edges. What was especially rough was that he had no filter on his mouth. Tammy and I were both scared and intimidated to ask him, but we did it anyway.

Coach Wilson lazily responded, "Well, we will have to see how strong you girls are first," followed by a big sigh. He rolled his eyes but we set up a date to try out for the team.

Soon after, Coach Wilson agreed to head up the first Bridge City High School girl's powerlifting team in the 1989-90 school year. I guess we must have impressed him. In the meantime, a few other brave girls decided to try out for the powerlifting team, too.

I excelled in powerlifting and loved the sport. I worked out super hard and I put all my heart in to being the best. My identity became solely wrapped up in my strength and how well I could perform as a powerlifter. I won the Texas State meet my junior year and won a National meet my senior year. My parents were so proud of me. Powerlifting made me feel tough and powerful. Looking back, I see that it caused me to embrace more of the masculine side of myself, while suppressing my feminine side. Unknowingly and unwillingly, I started rejecting my feminine self. I felt it was a weakness being a girl.

Quest for Acceptance

As a freshman, I finally had an older guy show interest in me. I was still so desperate to fit in and feel like "a normal girl." Having a boyfriend seemed like a good start. I wasn't even attracted to Alex but I started talking with him. I remember I begged my dad to drop me off at his house one evening. Dad didn't want to do that. Dad asked me repeatedly if his parents we're going to be there. I told him they would be. I really didn't know if his parents were going to be there or not. I didn't have a good feeling in my gut but I was determined to go.

Dad didn't speak to me the whole trip to Alex's house because he didn't want me to go. I just chalked it up as my dad being super protective of me. I wanted to have a boyfriend so badly that I was willing to go against both of our better judgements. I will never forget the look on my dad's face when he dropped me off. I didn't even know this guy, Alex.

From the moment I arrived, he was persistent in getting me to his bedroom. I didn't hardly know him and I don't remember him even talking to me. He immediately started forcing himself on me and his hands were all over me. I felt helpless and wanted to scream but I was scared to death. I didn't want to do this and I didn't know how to stop him. I hadn't ever experienced "a real kiss" from a guy at this point. After it was all over, I left his house feeling filthy. I couldn't look my dad in the eyes out of sheer shame because he was right about this guy. I never told anyone what had happened.

I arrived early to school the next day and Alex was waiting for me. He was hanging out around all his friends when he came up to me, pulled my face to his face and forced his tongue down my throat aggressively and tightly holding my face to his. I felt so violated. I wanted to go hide in a hole. I was so humiliated and shamed. I felt like a slut. Alex's friends were all snickering and laughing. I'm sure he had told all his friends that we had sex even though it wasn't ‌trve . I was a pure young girl and I had desired to stay that way until I got married.

Alex wasn't the only guy to force himself on me. A vicious cycle of guys sexually violating me continued throughout my early teenage years. One guy after another would step over my boundaries and force me to do things I didn't want to do. I never wanted to have encounters with these guys, yet I couldn't stand up for myself and I didn't know how to say no. I hated the way I this made me feel about myself. By this time, I despised guys and didn't feel safe with them or that I could trust them.

The rejection of my feminine side continued. When I was a senior in high school, I cut my hair short (probably to protect myself from predator-type guys). I remember one of the respected male football coaches at my high school started calling me "Butch" on a regular basis. He would say it as a joke and kind of laugh about it but I would cringe every time. I hated it because again, it made me feel "less than" a girl.

Looking for Love in All the Wrong Places

One night, when I was seventeen, my sister had something she was very scared to tell me. She opened up, cried her heart out, and confessed that she was secretly living a lesbian lifestyle. At the time, she was heartbroken over a break up with her girlfriend. I didn't know how to respond to her. I was confused. I cried with her and assured her of my love and acceptance. She was confused and terrified that our parents would find out her secret.

After her confession, I was a little relieved. I was struggling with my own "feminine identity" as a teenager and didn't know who I was. I ached to fit in and belong. At this point, I was so desperate that I didn't care what it looked like.

Later, my sister Melanie joined the Air Force. She never told Mom and Dad about being a lesbian out of fear. Prior to leaving for the Air Force, she somehow left a love letter in her pants pocket from her girlfriend. My mom found the letter a few days after Melanie left while washing her clothes. I was stuck with mom's plea for the truth about Melanie's secret lifestyle knowing that I was doing the same. I couldn't bear to tell her about my secrets, too. It tore me up to see my Mom in pieces over this. I couldn't stand the thought of hurting her any more so I kept it all bottled up inside for as long as I could.

After high school, my cousin Greg and I started going out to night clubs across the state line in Louisiana since the drinking age was eighteen. I started drinking and partying almost every night. I had no direction in my life. I started working at low end jobs. I worked two jobs, one of which was at a sandwich shop where I met three coworkers who professed their lesbian lifestyle publicly. They would openly share about their love affairs and all that was happening in their circle of friends which I soon joined. I was closest to Nicole.

They made me feel like I fit in and welcomed me with open arms so I started hanging out with them on a regular basis. Nicole flirted and showed interest in me. She frequently met up with my cousin and me at a night club in Louisiana. Even though I was still going out with guys and drinking a lot with my friends, I was curiously attracted to Nicole. Looking back, I was more attracted to being wanted, desirable, accepted, connected and safe because she was a woman.

Nicole and I eventually began meeting at a gay bar in Louisiana. Then, one fateful night, I willingly lost my innocence. I will never forget that night or rather the next morning. I felt shame and guilt and couldn't wait to leave the next morning because it felt so wrong. What was even more confusing was as wrong as that morning felt, there was a right feeling as well. It felt right to be connected, desired, noticed, accepted and safe. I was just looking for love in all the wrong places.

—3—

MY FIRST LOVE

Awakening

At nineteen, I met a woman who was involved in the Charismatic renewal within the Catholic Church. She invited me to attend one of their weekend retreats. I was intrigued because of the history of this movement. The Charismatic renewal was birthed around the 1960's and basically consisted of the mainstream Catholic congregations adopting beliefs and practices like that of the Pentecostals. Fundamental to the movement was the use of spiritual gifts including speaking in tongues, gifts of healing, prophecy, and dramatic encounters with God. This Charismatic movement moved throughout the Body of Christ with God's outpouring of His fire and power. Miraculous signs and wonders followed this movement and it is still burning bright within the Roman Catholic Church today all around the world.

Growing up in a traditional Catholic church, I didn't experience any manifestations of the Charismatic sort like speaking in tongues, words of knowledge, or prophetic words spoken over me. I had never seen people raise their hands and praise God until I was in high school at a Hot Hearts youth conference. Those things made me feel uncomfortable. It was foreign to me and I didn't understand it. I often thought, why would anyone do that?

I remember experiencing God's love in a mighty way when I received the sacrament of confirmation at sixteen years old. In hindsight, I know I received the release of the Holy Spirit but unfortunately, I didn't know what to do with it at the time. I wasn't taught how to live, grow, and move in the power of God's Spirit. No blame to anyone. One simply can't give what one doesn't have. I didn't know that I had many gifts from the Holy Spirit that were at my disposal anytime, anywhere and any place. I was taught about Charismatic gifts, but no one operated in them within my circle at church. Therefore, to me, it wasn't real or relevant. It was just a bunch of senseless stuff that happened way back in the book of Acts.

Back to the retreat weekend. I will never forget this retreat. It rocked me. I met Jesus and He wrecked me. The Charismatic Catholics who were leading this retreat were so happy. They glowed as they carried this overflowing joy that was contagious. They also had this strong sense of who they were. I thought to myself, I want what they have! I couldn't quite put my finger on it. All I knew was I had to have what they had.

One lady on the team gave a talk about receiving the baptism in the Holy Spirit. She explained speaking in tongues and other gifts you could receive from God. I desired everything that God had to give me and I figured if this is from God, it had to be good. These people were just too happy for it to be bad.

The last night at this retreat, I was super excited because I was going to be prayed over to receive the baptism of the Holy Spirit. The prayer teams were praying for a full release of all the gifts of the Holy Spirit within us and for God to fan them into flame. Wow! For the first time in my life I knew that God was alive and He really loved me. Jesus knew me by name and set a fire in my soul. I publicly accepted Jesus into my heart, and repented of all my sins.

Up to this point I felt conflicted about living the lesbian lifestyle. After I received this prayer, I had such a revelation that the lifestyle was not mine and the confusion was gone. It was washed away by the blood of Jesus. For the first time, I saw my sinfulness and my need for God's mercy and forgiveness. This was a love and acceptance I had never known before. God was so real and alive that I surrendered to Him that night. I experienced a deep desire to read the Bible, and for the first time the Bible came alive when I read it. I felt Jesus' love so deeply that it swept me off my feet. I literally could not feel my feet touching the floor when I took a step. I was so light and free. I was surrounded by God's peace and felt a renewed purpose for living and that was to live for Him.

I wanted and desired to give my all to Jesus. He gave His all to me so how could I deny my all to Him? His love was so sweet and tender that it drew me into this intimate relationship with Him. He would talk to me about everything. He desired me and I desired Him. I was never the same after this encounter with God. I looked for ways I could give my life and my all to Him and even started praying about becoming a nun. I started yearning to pledge vows to Jesus as a sister or nun. There was nothing than I wanted more than to be married to Jesus!

The Nestea Plunge

At age twenty-three, I entered a convent in Texas to see about a possible call to religious life. I entered this community as an aspirant. I vowed to live in community for six months in love, chastity and purity. This community was new and I visited it countless times before I made my decision to join. I was sure this one was it. It fit my personality perfectly and complimented all my gifts.

This community's charism was known as being the "Beloved Disciple" at the Feet of Jesus. They also believed and functioned in the gifts of the Spirit. It was normal for us to lift our hands and praise God in song and in tongues. The sisters and I were also part of a healing ministry that prayed for countless people at healing masses. Since this was a newly established community, there were only two sisters who were there prior to me joining making it just the three of us living in community together.

I had great expectations and my hopes were flying high. It was joy unspeakable! For the first time in my short life

I felt as though I had finally found my place and purpose in life. I fit in and was accepted with open arms. There was no doubt that God had called me there because I was able to live in complete abandon and surrender to Him.

After five months, I started to grow tired and weary. It seemed I had lost something along the way. I felt overloaded in different ministries and obligations and didn't have anyone to mentor me in my struggles of community life. I started losing sight of what my sole purpose was for living this life of sacrifice. Over a period of time, it seemed that I had no time to pray. When I did, I was too tired and would fall asleep. Eventually, I drifted away from intimacy with Jesus, the one true source of life to my soul.

Hidden Secrets

There were times, while still living in the convent, that I found myself feeling extremely weak. My flesh was rising up. Prior to my conversion, I had an addiction to alcohol. I had closed the door to alcohol when I gave my life to Jesus three years prior. The two sisters that directed the community were not aware of any of my past addictions and issues. I never felt called to tell them something that I felt that I was freed from.

The sisters and I enjoyed playing card games on the weekends. We would play for hours at a time and it was very relaxing and joyful. We started a habit of getting a six-pack of beer on occasion and I slowly opened the door to drinking again. Shortly thereafter, I went out with an old friend to a festival and I drank with him, too. Little by little, I swung the door open again to alcohol.

While living in community, I worked part time at a Christian daycare to help with finances. I was a Bible teacher at this daycare where I cared for almost thirty five-year olds. Throughout my time there I met some wonderful people. It was like a mission field of tiny people for me.

Over time, I became acquainted with all the teachers including Pam, who was one of the older teachers there. We would talk every day we worked together. She would tell me all her problems and would I share some of my story with her. Pam was married and over twice my age. In fact, her daughter was closer to my age than she was. Little by little, she wove her deception in from every angle. One day, she openly told me about the secret lesbian lifestyle she maintained while still married to her husband. She didn't see anything wrong with it. She even said her husband knew about it.

Pam knew I had vowed myself to God and I lived in a religious community discerning a call to be married to Jesus. Our friendship became complicated and dysfunctional quickly. I remember feeling pressured to call her. She convinced me that I wasn't a good friend if I didn't call or give her the attention she needed. There were days I would drive to a payphone at a park to call her. I felt obligated to call her yet guilty for doing so and I hated it. She was controlling and had a way of manipulating me to get what she wanted.

My biggest mistake was going to the beach with Pam's family for her daughter's birthday one weekend. I rode in the car with her to the beach and opened myself up even more to her including my past lesbian life. I drank a lot that weekend which didn't help things. We quickly developed an emotional dependency on top of the convoluted state we were already in. Next thing I knew, I was back in an emotional addiction and codependent relationship.

One thing led to another and our dependency became sexualized. How did I let this happen? I felt so guilty and trapped. No one could know about this. I told her several times I couldn't see her anymore, but it was complicated because I still worked with her at the daycare.

Beyond Repair

What was so clear to me before was just a big blur to me then. In condemnation, I felt there was no way out. Once again, I fell into a dark pit of confusion and deception. The two community sisters and I never discussed what was going on. I was so scared. I wanted to open my heart up to them, but I was terrified. I never talked about my struggles, my lesbian past, or my fear of men with the sisters. I kept that information completely covered up believing that it was the past and I was over it. I thought I was fine and I would just get over it. I didn't know that I needed healing from all my deep wounds.

All my hidden secrets were in the dark exactly where the enemy wanted them. The shame was tearing me up inside. I blocked parts of my story out because of the pain, and to this day I can hardly remember what happened the day I left the convent. What I do remember is the two sisters calling me aside for a meeting prior to me leaving. I was terrified. They must have known, I thought to myself. How could they know what was going on in my heart? I wanted to cry out for help but I was so afraid of judgement and rejection.

To the best of my memory, I remember them telling me I

had to leave. I wrote them a letter of apology while sobbing in my room the morning I left. The pain was so deep, it pierced my heart. The two sisters didn't know how to deal with my relational issues or my struggles. From what I could tell, they were trying to protect the community by preventing a scandal. It was easier to just let me go. It felt like a "don't ask, don't tell" kind of a situation.

The deepest wound for me was not having any closure. It was all left unsettled and unraveled in my heart. I left the convent feeling rejected, wounded, and lost. I believed I had failed God and the sisters whom I dearly loved. Everything I believed in was stripped away from me in one single day. My dreams were shattered and my spirit was crushed. I experienced John 10:10, where it says, *"The enemy comes only to steal, kill and destroy,"* [3] firsthand.

I stayed in that warped relationship with Pam for about six months after leaving the convent. I became so exhausted I felt like an empty corpse. I felt second best to her husband, and started feeling used in more ways than one. My soul became sickened by the lies and the guilt of meeting with her on occasional weekends. I tried numbing all the pain through drinking and having sex with Pam. I always returned home from my time with her with empty promises and a hollow heart. The guilt of having an affair with a married woman ate at my conscious like a cancer. I must have ended it a dozen times before it was finally over.

At twenty-five, I still had no sense of direction for my life. I tossed to and fro, back and forth, in and out of the lesbian lifestyle. I would get emotionally and sexually involved with a woman then God would convict my heart and I would acknowledge that it was wrong. I repeated this vicious cycle of destruction over and over again.

Surrendered to the Lifestyle

It seemed that I could not find my way out of the lesbian lifestyle, and at this point, I didn't want out. I loved it too much. I loved women. I loved everything about this lifestyle. I liked the way it made me feel emotionally, sexually, and personally and I felt safe with women. I took pride in being a lesbian. It became my identity. It was a defining factor in everything I was, what I did, who I hung out with, how I dressed and looked, how I cut my hair, how I carried myself etc. Being a lesbian became entwined in the very fabric of my being and my existence. I embraced it and decided it was who I was. Being a lesbian made me feel tough, powerful, dominant and unstoppable, although buried deep down, I still had a dream of getting married to a man and having beautiful children one day even though I didn't trust men.

At age twenty-nine, I met a woman at work named Lori. Lori was my direct manager at a distribution warehouse. Lori moved to Texas from her hometown in Georgia to help with the opening of a new warehouse in Texas. I was immediately attracted to her kind heart and charismatic personality.

As co-workers, we were forbidden to associate with one another outside of work because of her management position. Eventually we went around the rule with the help of my friends. Lori and I immediately connected on a deep emotional level and shared a kindred spirit. It didn't take long for me to know she was "the one." I moved in with her soon after we met and life was good. I had never felt this way before about anyone.

I once brought Lori over to my parents' house while we lived in Texas. It was about a two-hour drive home and I was nervous about it. Mom and Dad knew she was my girlfriend but we never talked about it. They acted civil to her, however, it still felt cold. Their treatment of her made me regret taking her home. I was so embarrassed and hurt that I cried the whole way back, apologizing to Lori.

I just wanted them to see her gentle and loving heart the way I did. I never tried to push my lifestyle or girlfriends down their throats. I was already aware of their feelings toward our relationship and my lifestyle. Obviously, they didn't agree or accept it. My lifestyle caused a rift in my relationship with my parents which hurt deeply. We grew distant and didn't share anything that was really personal or intimate. Once again, it felt like more rejection.

After living with Lori in Texas for a year, we both decided to move back to her hometown in Georgia. Lori missed her family and I thought it would be the perfect new beginning for us. We never discussed getting married but I was already wedded to her in my heart. Lori still owned a home in Georgia and her family accepted our relationship. Lori and I never really discussed it, but I figured it would be easier for us to have a life together where people would accept us.

Lori and I still worked for the same company, but her transfer paperwork came through before mine did. I moved her back home to Georgia with all our belongings and planned to follow as soon as my transfer was complete. My thought for this trip was to stay a couple of nights at her house in Georgia to help get things in order before I went back to Texas. For some reason my job transfer was taking longer than normal to be processed.

4

CORNERED BY GRACE

"From the creation to the cross,
Then from the cross into eternity,
Your grace finds me,
Yes, your grace finds me."[4] -Matt Redman

My Last Night in Georgia

September 29, 2003 was my last night in Georgia with Lori before flying back to Texas the next morning. I had just fallen asleep when something gently but firmly woke me up. I sensed a strong presence in the room where Lori and I were sleeping. She was still asleep while I felt drawn to look up towards the left side of the corner wall. To my amazement, there was the Blessed Virgin Mary in all white with her arms outstretched to me. I felt total peace while God's love and mercy washed over me wave after wave. Tears trailed down my face as God's grace flooded my soul in an instant and took my breath away.

Then Mary came right before me, and her face was extremely sad. She looked into my eyes trying to desperately warn me and shouted into my spirit, "No, this cannot be!" Her intense gaze shook me to the core and echoed loudly through every fiber of my being. I could tell she was frightened and concerned for me. At that moment, I had no doubt that what I was doing was wrong.

I was up all night long as my heart was being softened by the love of Jesus. The presence of God was so tangible that I couldn't stop the tears from flowing. I was once again overwhelmed by Jesus' love and faithfulness to me despite my current condition. He reached out once again and invaded the core of my heart.

God's Beloved?

"I've been hiding,
Afraid I've let you down.
But in your eyes,
There's only grace now."[5] -Lauren Daigle

I laid there in bed simply awestruck thinking about all that had just occurred. My mind was racing out of shock that God could still see me as "His Beloved." The Virgin Mary came down from Heaven to give me a message while I'm in the middle of this?! I think I somehow caught a glimpse of how Elizabeth must have felt in the Bible when Mary visited her. In Luke 1:43, Elizabeth says,

"But why am I so favored, that the mother of my Lord should come to me?" [6] I kept thinking the same thing. Why am I so favored? Why am I so loved? That's how mind-blown I was.

I was humbled in the deepest way possible, especially knowing that I had just finished having sexual relations with Lori minutes before this miracle happened. I felt I was filthy, guilty, and certainly unworthy. I didn't deserve to be loved like that particularly since I didn't even ask to be pursued in such a big way. After all, I wasn't even seeking God.

God came to me and met me in my bed that night. Heaven came down to me in that room. I didn't want or ask God to reveal Himself and shower me with His mercy and grace. As a matter of fact, I didn't want to "see" the truth. The truth demanded a response. Jesus' love beckons a response. I encountered the living God! His love overtook my very existence. I sensed a deep conviction of what was right and what was wrong. I knew that I had to leave my relationship with Lori for Jesus. I loved Lori with all that was in me. I didn't know how I was going to be able to do it and I knew I couldn't do it on my own, but I knew I had to. The very thought of leaving her broke my heart but I knew this was the decision I had to make for truth, for Jesus. It was all about Him. I chose Jesus.

There were moments while living with Lori, where I felt deeply convicted of sexual sin and I knew it was because my parents were praying for me. I know their prayers moved God's heart, and that made me angry. In total rebellion, I once raised my fist to heaven and demanded that she stop praying for me! I wasn't against praying in general, but I didn't have any desire to change my lifestyle. I really wanted to be left alone to live the way I wanted and with whom I wanted.

The night seemed like it lasted for an eternity. Occasionally, I glanced at Lori sleeping. Tears streamed down my face because deep down I knew what I had to do. I was wide awake until dawn. My mind was racing with thoughts of, "How could I let her go? She is my life." There was no logical reason to leave her. She was good to me. Up until then, I wanted to share the rest of my life with her. I was certain of that.

Morning finally arrived.

Lori looked into my eyes and said, "Good morning, Dana."

I could barely look her in the eyes and I certainly couldn't hold my tears back.

"Are you okay?" she said, with a concerned look in her eyes.

I could only sigh.

She said, "Dana, are you nervous about flying home to Texas?"

I could hardly hold it together and wasn't ready to tell her I was leaving her.

Jump Start

I will never forget the morning I boarded the plane to fly back to Texas. Lori thought I was just sad to leave for a few weeks. My plan to spend the rest of my life with her was radically changed. Throughout my flight, the Holy Spirit and all the grace from the heavenly encounter stayed with me in a very deep way. God was after me. I was cornered by His grace and mercy. There was no way out of His love and I finally didn't want out.

I had forgotten my first love, like it talks about in Hosea 2:7, until this encounter happened. Flashes of the Virgin Mary's face would rise up in my spirit and give me a spiritual jolt. It physically felt like a shock to my heart, like when paramedics are forced to use a defibrillator to "jump-start" failed hearts in an emergency crisis. This was my jump-start.

Things of God that I had unconsciously blocked out of my mind and heart started surfacing again. Holy thoughts and scriptures were coming to my memory. It was like I had "spiritual amnesia" before and suddenly it was all coming back to me. Scriptures from the Bible speaking of God's love were flooding my mind as well as true purpose and identity statements like, "I have called you by name, Dana. You are mine. I love you, Dana. You are my beloved daughter. You are chosen to be a child of the light. You are My Beloved, Dana. My Spirit has anointed you to do mighty things in my name, to bring sight to the blind, liberty to captives. I have a plan for you, a divine plan to bring my Kingdom to earth in my glory and truth." It was becoming clear to me that I had centered my entire existence and meaning of my life around my lesbian identity and my relationship with Lori.

The flight continued with remarkably intense thoughts and feelings. I experienced a deep sense of urgency and revelation of truth that coursed through my heart. This deep conviction of right and wrong came over me and the urgency to choose life or death was startling. I experienced a holy fear of God while flying back to Texas.

Jesus was present with me and He made an invitation to truth and love just for me.

Up to this point, I had all of this hidden in my heart and still hadn't repented. Romans 2:4 says, *"Or do you think lightly of the riches of His kindness and tolerance and patience, not knowing that the kindness of God leads you to repentance?"[7]* I was wrestling with God. I was the kind of person who gave her all and when I put my heart into something, I was all in. My heart was still entangled in my relationship with Lori. But it began to feel like a tug of war because God was pulling on the other end.

Once I arrived back in Texas, I didn't dare tell anyone of my heavenly visitation. It only took a few days until I couldn't stand it any longer. I was about to pop. I knew the validity of why I should tell someone what was happening in my heart and about the miracle that had taken place. Yet I was terrified and too frightened to open up.

I stayed with a work-friend until my job transfer was complete to move to Georgia. On my first day back at work, I couldn't hold it in any longer. I told her about the miracle that had happened to me in Georgia. Tears welled up in her eyes and she had this look of amazement on her face. She listened to my heart and was deeply touched.

Brick Wall

Hosea 2:6 says, *"Therefore I will block her path with thorn bushes, I will block her path with a wall so that she cannot find her way."*[8]

On my second day back at work, I was in the receiving department minding my own business when I received a phone call from the HR office.

The representative said, "Dana, your transfer paperwork is final. Can you come to the office and sign for your transfer to Georgia?"

"Sure," I said.

I started to tremble and my heart was racing. I had already made a commitment to Lori and she was waiting for me in Georgia. I couldn't let her down, I simply had to go. Nobody was going to stop me. I started to make my way down to the HR office. I started walking down the hallway in receiving when something stopped me in my tracks. I physically felt this ten foot brick wall in front of me. I was unable to move forward.

At that moment, I just fell on the floor. I broke. I cried out to God. (Thank God no one was around, or so I like to think anyways.) After laying there for a few minutes, all I could think of was my mom. I pulled myself up and dashed to the receiving phone in the back. Mom and I weren't on the best of terms at the time. There was a lot of friction and distance between us because of my lifestyle. I would have to suck up my pride to call her and tell her what had happened in Georgia because that would be admitting that I was wrong all along and that she was right. Despite how much I didn't want to do that, I had to call my mom. What made it even more difficult was that I hadn't had the heart to tell her I was moving to Georgia with Lori, so I had sent her the news in a letter a few months previous.

My heart was still beating fast and I was almost at the point of hyperventilating. I reluctantly dialed, and to my chagrin, she answered the phone.

"Mom?" I said.

There was a long silence. We small talked a little. I couldn't hold it in any longer. I told her the miracle that had happened in Georgia. I remember hearing the phone fall to the floor and all I could hear was her sobbing in the background. It made me choke up. Mom finally came back to the phone and we talked more.

She said, "I prayed for a miracle, Dana. I prayed for God to send His mother to you."

My heart was broken and my dreams were shattered. How was I going to tell Lori that I could not be with her? I moved back to Texas but could never actually tell Lori it was over. I couldn't do it. My heart couldn't take it. As time went on, it was the grace of God that kept me from going back to her.

In a moment of weakness, I couldn't bear the torment and pain in my heart any longer. After three months of staying away, I drove sixteen hours to her hometown in Georgia to surprise her on December 23 for Christmas. She was furious that I showed up at her home without telling her I was coming. She held nothing but anger towards me for the pain that I had caused her. I left her house heartbroken once again.

Angry at the World

"We can't always prevent painful experiences from happening, but we can keep the pain from continuing.

When we begin dwelling on our pain, we give the devil an opportunity to wound us."⁹ Mike Purkey

As time went on, my heart became progressively harder and harder. It became like stone with a ten-foot wall around it. I didn't know how to cope or deal with the loss of Lori, so I let the grief overcome me. I could hardly function in daily life. I was so deeply wounded that I could only focus on one thing: my pain. I began to question, "God, why can't I just be with Lori? Where are you God? Do you even care? Do you even see my shattered heart?"

Because the anguish and pain I was experiencing wasn't dealt with, I soon became embittered against God. I started to direct my pain towards God like a weapon and grew angry towards Him. Little did I know that this was just another tool in the devil's bag to wound me on a deeper level.

Eventually, I stopped asking God for help and leaned on my own strength to cope and survive. I started drinking again every night to numb the pain. I became excessive in my training for long distance running, exhausting and abusing my body until I couldn't physically go anymore. I started going back to the gay bars looking for affection and attention. I still loved Lori so my heart couldn't bear the thought of sleeping with someone else. I felt like I had no one to open my heart up to and nowhere to grieve. I needed a safe place to mourn and I felt the "church" wouldn't be able to understand or acknowledge the sincerity of my sorrow and grief over a woman.

Because I felt so alone in my pain I became bitter at the church, my family and just at life in general. "To hell with everyone," became my attitude. I didn't even care anymore. I was so tired of rejection, pain and loss. No one was going to be able hurt me anymore. No one, not even God. I was a tough girl. It was really pride and arrogance, thinking I could be "self-sufficient". I lived only for the moment and my heart grew colder and colder.

I turned away from God again, and after six months of living this way, I started having casual sex with a girlfriend. I continued on this path of destruction, satisfying my needs and suppressing my pain with drinking, sex and clubbing, and even popping pills with my alcohol on occasion. This time I lived with reckless abandon, running as fast as my feet could carry me, further and further away from God. I ran away from God and soon squandered all my inheritance from my wild living as a prodigal.

My heart became obstinate toward God like a hardened reprobate. At this point, I entered into a deeper level of rebellion. I continued running away from my Heavenly Father who continuously pursued me with His mercy and love. God permitted me to do it my way but there were severe consequences for the choices I made for my life. There was a series of traumatic events that took place during this time and God had to literally break my pride to get me to truly surrender.

5

The Dark Night

"In the darkness... Lord, my God, who am I that you should forsake me?
The child of your love- and now become as your most hated one.
The one- you have thrown away as unwanted-unloved.
I call, I cling, I want, and there is no one to answer."[10]
– Saint Mother Teresa

Cry for Help

February 16, 2005, was what I now call "The Dark Night." I was in the middle of a wild and rebellious phase, and went to a local gay bar in Houston with my friend, Rhonda, to shoot pool and drink beer. As we were playing, I noticed cuts on her arm. It appeared that she had been cutting herself. I questioned her about the marks and she immediately tried to deny and distract me from the question. Out of genuine concern for her, I persisted with my questioning. Rhonda never gave me an honest explanation. I remember her previously mentioning there was some traumatic sexual abuse she had endured as a child but I wasn't sure if that was the cause.

After we left the bar, we headed back to the apartment. I couldn't shake the thoughts of her cutting herself so I offered to pray with her and thankfully she agreed. I started praying for her on the fourth level of our high-rise balcony apartment. My girlfriend, Jennifer, was in bed sleeping in the apartment while all this was taking place. After I started praying for Rhonda, she started trying to hit me with a stick of some sort and then tried to attack me. I was scared for me *and* for her. She sounded out of her mind with all of the disturbing things she was saying. She threatened to take her life by going into oncoming traffic while driving. She couldn't really look me in the eyes or focus on anything.

This crazed behavior continued for about 20 minutes. I could tell this wasn't simply depression or a need for attention, it was a spiritual battle within her. Although my dad and I didn't talk much at this time, I knew I had to call him. I needed sound advice and spiritual wisdom. I was scared for Rhonda and the safety of others. I told my dad what was going on. He advised me to stop praying for her at this point, so I did.

He asked, "Dana do you have your Bible?"

At this time in my life, I didn't even know where my Bible was located. My dad prayed for both Rhonda and me.

Rhonda finally calmed down but she was not ok, and truthfully, I was not ok either. The whole thing was so violent, traumatic and scary. Rhonda left quite late that night while I crumbled, feeling alone and helpless in my efforts to help her.

I was determined to find help for Rhonda. I called a dozen churches (Catholic and Protestant alike) in the area and literally no one would help me. I called friends from home, two hours away even. I drove her from Houston to my hometown of Bridge City, Texas, and a local prayer group prayed for her yet she still wasn't free. This continued to go on and her condition became worse and worse. Again, she would tell me she heard voices telling her to get into oncoming traffic while driving and so much more. What made my position even more challenging was that no one else knew about her situation. I felt trapped, alone, and powerless. There were several instances where she could have hurt me or possibly even killed me at times. I became desperate for help.

Again, I reached out to several more churches and everyone seemed too busy to help me. I finally contacted an older friend of my family, Dr. Willie Andrepont DDS, whose dental practice was in Groves, TX. He was a Charismatic Catholic who would often pray for the deliverance and healing of the tormented. Dr. Willie immediately agreed to pray for Rhonda over the phone.

While I wanted so desperately to help Rhonda get delivered, I, myself, was not well and needed help. My whole life was filled with chaos charging in from every direction. By this point, I was at my wits' end and my stress level was tipping the scales. All coping mechanisms were completely tapped out and I had started to feel out of control.

We set up a time for her prayer before the week was over. Dr. Willie prayed for over two hours for Rhonda over the phone while I was in the room with her. It was intense and exhausting. To make matters worse, the phone kept disconnecting the call, at least a dozen times while he was praying, and I had to keep redialing.

After hours of prayer and intercession, she was finally set free! She glowed with the light of Jesus in that room. She was laughing again like she was a little girl. The presence of God was so strong that the room felt like an oven. The fire of God was so evident that her mom and sister came upstairs and they didn't even know what was taking place. They both started crying because they were touched by the tangible presence of God. They came into the room, started hugging Rhonda and crying with us over all that God had done. It was joyous! Jesus set Rhonda free that night!

Unveiled Scales

When I went back to my apartment that evening following Rhonda's deliverance, I started experiencing extreme fear. The enemy started tormenting me. It was like there was a new level of darkness in me that I immediately recognized because I had just seen the same darkness come out of Rhonda. I could see my sin before my eyes. I could see my selfishness, pride, arrogance, and my rebellious spirit. Just like in the book of Acts, it was as if the scales of deception fell from my eyes and I was deeply convicted of my engagement in sexual sin.

I fell to my knees before the Lord in my apartment and cried out to Him. Immediately, I felt God instruct me to go to confession and repent of living in sexual sin. I was desperate to confess my sin to someone. The next day, I went to the closest Catholic church. Thankfully, the priest was hearing confessions that afternoon.

As I was waiting in line for the priest to hear my confession, I experienced an aggressive tug-of-war inside of my heart. It was a physical manifestation of the demonic within my heart and in my body. It tormented me and it physically wouldn't let me go in my heart. The closer it came for the priest to hear my confession, the tougher and stronger this tugging became. It even got to the point where it felt extremely violent. This was a battle taking place within my heart and soul.

When I finally reached the confessional, I just threw myself on the floor and wailed out to God for His mercy and grace. I didn't care who was around, I just gave it all to Jesus. I threw myself on His mercy seat. I was undone. I knew it was over. I could finally see everything for what it was and I could separate the truth from the lies regarding sexual sin again. All the scales that were blinding me from seeing the truth of my "selfish ways" were unveiled in that instant.

I had to make some serious decisions concerning my life, especially Jennifer, my girlfriend who I had been living with for a year now. I immediately told her everything about Rhonda and what happened to me. I told her about my awakening, my conversion story that literally just happened that day. She wanted to believe me, but it was a bit much for her to take in. Although it was a lot for her to digest, she trusted me. I told her I couldn't be with her anymore, that the most we could ever be was friends, and that it was going to change everything in our relationship.

At first, Jennifer didn't particularly like the choice I made towards God. It drastically affected her life, our relationship, and everything that we shared. She soon started to poke fun at me for being in church every day. I was going because I was still experiencing horrific torment from the enemy. My coping mechanisms were gone. My stressors were capped. I was emotionally tapped out.

Although I was temporarily relieved after my confession and repentance, I still felt a physical manifestation in my heart. It was so painful, heavy and dark. I felt no peace in my mind and body. After praying in the room for Rhonda, I literally felt like I was spiritually invaded. This darkness entered my heart, my mind and my body without permission. The enemy was fighting for my soul causing me to have extreme terror. I soon started having panic attacks on a regular basis. My condition was worsening and I could no longer function in everyday normal circumstances. I couldn't bear to be in a crowd of people or carry on a simple conversation, or go in to a grocery store without having severe panic attacks.

Within a week, Jennifer soon started to experience terror and sleeplessness as well. She said she felt like she was going to go crazy and could barely make it to work. She was experiencing some of the same things I was except hers wasn't as severe. One day I heard her crying out to Jesus in our apartment. I had a Sacred Heart of Jesus picture hanging on our wall. She pulled that picture of Jesus off the wall and was crying out while holding that picture to her chest. I will never forget the cry she expressed to Jesus that day. In that same week, Jennifer threw out her stash of marijuana joints, secular cd's and everything that she felt was opposed to God. I watched her as she went out to the dumpster and threw it all away. She asked me to take her to church. She started going to daily mass with me at the Catholic Church down the road. Soon after, she started going to classes with me to learn more about Catholicism and study the Word of God.

I experienced night terrors for a straight year following

the dark night. When I did fall asleep for brief moments, I would dream that this evil man was chasing after me and I was constantly running from him all night long. He had a gun and wanted to kill me. Every time he would catch up to me, I would see him aim his gun at me and I would barely make my way out of it. He was after me. He wanted to destroy me. He wanted me dead. I was running for my life, and was scared to death that he would finally catch me and kill me.

Blind Faith

"Our faith begins at the point where atheists suppose that it must end. Our faith begins with the bleakness and power which is the night of the cross, abandonment, temptation, and doubt about everything that exists! Our faith must be born where it is abandoned by all tangible reality; it must be born of nothingness, it must taste this nothingness and be given it to taste in a way no philosophy of nihilism can imagine." [11] *–Jurgen Moltmann*

Six months into these night terrors, I went to a weekend retreat at the Catholic Charismatic Center in Houston, Texas. I vividly remember this retreat. I remember the speaker talking on the scripture in 2 Corinthians 5:7

which says, *"For we walk by faith, not by sight."*[12] Throughout the course of the retreat, the leaders did an exercise of faith by blindfolding us. Once we all put our blindfolds on, the director of the retreat told us to start taking steps. I remember thinking this is exactly how I felt without the blindfold on.

The director told us, "Just trust Jesus."

She asked us again to start taking steps with our eyes blindfolded. Tears streamed down my face because this exercise highlighted the pain I was already in: blinded and terrified in this darkness.

She said, "Just trust Jesus. He will lead you."

As I was proceeding to take steps slowly, I tangibly felt someone physically holding me and guiding me. I felt God's presence. I felt Him. God was holding me. I just wept and was so relieved by His presence in this moment. I left that retreat knowing God was with me no matter how dark it was.

I continued seeking help and people who could pray for me. I went to church almost every opportunity possible. I received Holy Communion every day at Holy Mass and it gave me consolation. Receiving Jesus in Holy

Communion was the only relief from the torment in my mind and body that was like hell on earth.

I started fasting three to four times a week on bread and water and praying for God to breakthrough and deliver me. I would search out homeless people and bring them food on the streets of Houston, Texas where I was living. Jennifer and I would sit with them in the streets and give them comfort and words of encouragement. We became deeply involved with some of them. It was healing for me. I realized I wasn't the only one in the world who was suffering. In this season, God gave me a deep hunger to give consolation to the helpless and homeless. I wanted to soothe their pain in some way. I know I didn't have much to give but I gave them what I had—hope in Jesus.

I was so desperate to experience God's peace again. I stayed on my face before Him because for me, there was no other way to survive. It was life or death for me. I fought with every fiber of my being against this assault for my life. I battled. The enemy wasn't going to take me out without a fight. I was sure that my God was going to come through for me. I didn't know when or how I would get relief, but I started standing on His Word.

I rose as a warrior for my very life. I had a fight rise in me that I never knew I had. Really it was God who was rising in me. Romans 8:31 says, *"If God is for us, who can be against us?"*[13] All the demons in hell can come against us or our loved ones, but we have a God who is mighty to save!

I went through this dark night season feeling like I was riding a roller coaster. I felt like Job did in the Bible. The book of Job tells us about his story. The devil caused Job's troubles but Job didn't know this fact.[14] Job thought that God caused the problems.[15] In fact, God did not cause Job's troubles but He did permit Job to suffer through them. Still, Job turned to God and refused to insult God.[16]

Like Job, I sought the Lord! I knew He was the one to deliver me. I knew He was the one to pull me out of this miry pit. Although I had glimpses of light and hope, I still doubted and questioned God: HOW? WHEN? WHY? I would ask these questions repeatedly. I was plagued by these questions: How are you going to heal me? When are you going to deliver me? Why do I have to suffer in this way for this long? Why the silence from God for so long? And just like Job, I didn't understand. Time stood still through this season of suffering. I prayed to God that

He would heal, deliver, and restore all that the enemy had stolen from me. My life, as I knew it before, was gone.

Post-Traumatic Stress Disorder

Everyday life and its tasks became overwhelming. To simply get in my car and go to the grocery store was a challenge for me. I didn't want to go to the doctor to get treated because I didn't want to get hooked on a drug, but at this point I felt had no choice.

My symptoms became so severe that I had to get medical help. I was still not sleeping at night. I experienced severe sleep deprivation to the point where I feared for my life. I didn't know if I would make it from minute to minute. It had been years since the spiritual attack occurred and I was tired of this vicious cycle. I went through several medications for depression and anxiety including one that caused me to experience severe depressions, all the while still drowning in hopelessness and despair.

In the fall of 2006, I read a book, *Embracing the Wounds of Post-Traumatic Stress Disorder*. The Holy Spirit guided me to this book while I was working part-time at a local Christian bookstore. I finally realized that I had experienced trauma during Rhonda's deliverance. However, my trauma was not exclusively from that event. It was also deeply connected to a long series of losses I had been through. I lost my friends, girlfriends, health, sense of safety and well-being, my identity, social structure, independence, self-esteem and possibly my financial security since I didn't know if I would be able to continue to work in that state of mind.

Before this tragedy, I was a very active, high-energy person who could coordinate many different functions at work with no worries. I was an athlete and trained hard for long distance running. I was an extremely fit and social person. Now, I couldn't even carry on a simple conversation or be in a crowd of people because of this anxiety disorder.

The emotional pain from the disorder was horrific. It took a hold of my life and it didn't let up. I didn't understand what I was going through at the time, I just knew I wanted to "go back" to normal life, whatever that was. I could still physically feel the enemy fighting for my soul even though deep within I knew that God was greater and that His resurrection power lived inside of me! 1 John 4:4 says, *"Ye are of God, little children, and have overcome them: Because greater is He that is in you, than he that is in the world."[17]*

One day while I was on my lunch break, I went to the Adoration Chapel by my work since I was fasting. I fell on my face before God. My prayer mostly consisted of crying out to God. I didn't have words for anything. It was truly a heart cry from the depths of my soul. While I was sobbing to Jesus, I immediately sensed His mercy and blood washing over my whole body. The presence of God was palpable and was cleansing me like never before. I felt a holy remorse for all my sins and my rebellion. I was so sorry. I couldn't look up or get up because the glory of God was so strong.

The mercy of Jesus continued to flow and wash me for about thirty minutes. During this encounter, I received Psalm 51 from the Lord. At the time, I didn't even know what this particular Psalm was about. When I was finally able to get up off the floor, I immediately looked up Psalm 51:1-16 and read that it was a psalm of David, when Nathan the prophet came to him after his affair with Bathsheba. It reads:

> *"Have mercy on me, God, in your goodness; in your abundant compassion blot out my offense. Wash away all my guilt; from my sin cleanse me. For I know my offense; my sin is always before me. Against you alone have I*

sinned; I have done such evil in your sight that you are just in your sentence, blameless when you condemn. True, I was born guilty, a sinner, even as my mother conceived me. Still, you insist on sincerity of heart; in my inmost being teach me wisdom. Cleanse me with hyssop, that I may be pure; wash me, make me whiter than snow. Let me hear sounds of joy and gladness; let the bones you have crushed rejoice. Turn away your face from my sins; blot out all my guilt. A clean heart create for me, God; renew in me a steadfast spirit. Do not drive me from your presence, nor take from me your Holy Spirit. Restore my joy in your salvation; sustain in me a willing spirit. I will teach the wicked your ways, that sinners may return to you. Rescue me from death, God, my saving God, that my tongue may praise your healing power."[18]

Left for Dead

"Even when we're responsible for the terrible spiritual condition in which we find ourselves, Jesus still sees us through His eyes of compassion and meets us where we are."[19] -Mike Purkey

As of January 2007, I was still dealing with extreme torment and dread and only getting enough sleep to survive. It seemed like my condition was getting worse. I was completely filled with darkness and uncontrollable thoughts raced violently in my mind. I believed for sure that I was going to die. The thoughts and accusations from the enemy were not just thoughts anymore. I began to believe and come into agreement with all the enemy's lies and accusations. They became my reality. Unfortunately, because I believed the enemy's lies, it gave him power that was not rightfully his. I had webs of deception entangling my mind. The enemy had a death grip wrapped around me like a python wraps his prey. The enemy's tactic was to torment me until I came in to complete agreement with him and to continue to destroy and scare me so I would stay locked down with terror.

He was after my life in full force. He was relentless in his pursuit to kill me because he wanted to take me out. I'm certain of that. The enemy came to steal, kill and destroy all that was left in me.[20] I never wanted to physically kill myself, but I thought if Jesus would take me home, I wouldn't be here in this agony of hell. I wished that would happen. I even fantasized about what it would be like to die and go to heaven because I didn't know how much more I could take.

In Mark 5:1-5, there is the account of the man with the evil spirits that came from the tomb to meet Jesus. The man was suffering terribly because these spirits were controlling his mind and body and nothing could keep him calm. He was tormented night and day and he screamed among the tombs and in the hills. When the man saw Jesus from a long way off, he ran to him and fell on his knees in front of Jesus. I could relate to that possessed man and his cries of, *"Jesus, save me! Jesus, deliver me! Abba Father!"[21]* I begged God to set me free.

Like the man from the tombs, I still had a flicker of hope left in me. It was "faith as small as a mustard seed."[22] My faith was small, but I still believed that somehow God was going to breakthrough this dark night of me living among the tombs. In the Gospel, the man's hands and feet had often been chained and no one could contain him. Although I physically didn't have chains holding me down, the enemy had me bound in my heart and mind.

Through this darkness, I still believed that Jesus was going to come and calm my stormy seas that raged inside of me: fear, despair, hopelessness, and death. I was drowning and the waves were crashing in on me. I had no control over my life, my thoughts, and my existence. I cried night and day, day and night out to God.

Could anyone hear my cry for help? Could anyone see that I was dying on the side of the road? Luke 10:30-35 is a parable about the Good Samaritan and also of the lonely man walking down the road to Jericho. It says, *"A certain man went down from Jerusalem to Jericho, and fell among thieves, who stripped him of his clothing, wounded him, and departed, leaving him half dead."*[23] I felt like this man, too. He was helpless, wounded, beaten, bleeding, and left half-dead. I felt like a wounded animal left for dead in the wilderness with vultures hovering over me waiting for my death to come quickly.

6

Rope of Hope

"Hope is being able to see that there is light despite all of the darkness."[24] *-Desmond Tutu*

Unbound

God knew that I needed my own Good Samaritan. He knew I needed someone to help me in my healing process. I could only get so much breakthrough on my own. I needed someone from the Body of Christ to intervene. John 11:43 is the account of Jesus raising Lazarus from the dead. *"When He had said this, Jesus called in a loud voice, 'Lazarus, Come out!' The dead man came out, his hands and feet wrapped with strips of linen, and a cloth around his face. Jesus said to them, 'Take off the grave clothes and let him go.'"*[25]

Like Lazarus, Jesus called me out of the grave (sexual sin) and in to life. Although I walked out of the tomb (sin) like Lazarus, I was still bound and all tied up with grave clothes. The scripture says that he also had a cloth around his face. Although Lazarus was alive, he couldn't see. Lazarus needed help. Jesus raised him from the dead and called him out his tomb, but Jesus commissioned the community of people to untie him and let him go.

Imagine this scenario playing out: Lazarus had been dead for three days. He smelled horribly, probably bad enough to make people not want to get near him let alone touch him to unwrap him. He was nasty and likely unpleasant to look at. How many of us would try to find anything else to do rather than get our hands dirty when someone needs help? If it inconveniences us in the least bit, we turn our backs and look the other way.

We can see this avoidance behavior replicated with the homeless who carry a pungent, unpleasant odor. It's understandable why few end up being any kind of help to them because it messes with us. It makes us ask all kinds of questions in our minds about how they ever let themselves get this way and all the possible decisions they could have made differently. Jesus identifies these people and other social rejects as the "least of these" and reminds us that they are still visible and important to Him. Matthew 25:40 says, *"The King will reply, 'Truly I tell you, whatever you did for one of the least of these brothers and sisters of mine, you did for me.'"*[26]

This is one of the key instructions for the body of Christ to remember and focus on for there to be any kind of revival today. God is asking us to care for "the least of these" who need a Good Samaritan to come alongside them, take off the grave clothes that bind them, mend their wounds and demonstrate God's healing love and compassion. This is exactly the tender love I needed for my inner healing to manifest.

God sent amazing men and women to minister to me throughout my journey of healing and deliverance. I believe God hand-picked the people to minister to me in my brokenness and renewed identity. I reached out to Father Mark, a priest friend of mine from long ago. He lived in San Antonio, Texas and was like a father to me. I explained to him what I was going through and he graciously invited me to come visit for a few days. During that time, he prayed for my complete deliverance and healing and towards the end of our prayer, Father Mark had a vision of what had taken place during my prayer time. Father Mark saw a hook that resembled the one that Captain Hook had as a hand. This hook was lodged in my heart. Father Mark saw God's hand come down from Heaven and gently pull that hook completely out of my heart.

After this took place, I physically felt a release within my heart. The tugging and pulling feelings I had experienced in my heart finally stopped. The physical pain from all that emotional torment was gone as well. It was a miracle. I finally had a peace in my heart I didn't have before. It made more sense now why I could not find comfort or relief because this hook was still there. The revelation that came through prayer was that the hook represented the deep spiritual bond or soul tie I had in my heart with Lori, my ex-girlfriend from Georgia. I know I am not the only one who has experienced this kind of pain before. It is my prayer for anyone in the midst of this type of suffering gain insight as to its source and the people to surround you and pray you through.

I know now that I gave the enemy access to my heart in several different ways while living as a prodigal. One way I opened the door was in giving myself away to so many different lovers throughout my life. Another way was through my off and on struggle with alcohol addiction. By this time in my life, I had given sin so many pathways in that it felt like a hopeless battle. The enemy had wide open access to my heart and was using it because I continued to choose a life of sin and not God's way. After so many years of living in sexual sin and darkness, I basically created a home for the enemy while pushing Jesus out little by little. I couldn't see it at the time, but I see now the consequences for the decisions I was making.

Over time, I had unknowingly developed strongholds of sin and addictions. These two forces usually don't just go away overnight or without a fight. Through the blood of Jesus, they can be broken immediately but removing them is a process that requires a constant "YES" to God on our part to desire freedom and wholeness.

When left unchecked and buried, strongholds and addictions become so integrated with your identity that they can seem to be part of you. The truth is that they don't alter your true identity but rather they bend and manipulate you into a false or altered version of self.

It can sometimes take time for strongholds to be rendered powerless in your life. In my case, it was a process. Even though I had just repented and confessed sexual sin, the enemy didn't want to let me go that easy. He attacked me in other areas like my mind with fear, terror, and torment.

I lived in this dark night phase for two years. During that time, I learned an incredible lesson that brought me to a place of surrender and obedience to Jesus Christ. I even wrote it in my journal: "Don't play with fire unless you want to get burned." I brought much of this pain onto myself through my previous choices. But at this point, I desired to walk in complete obedience to Jesus because all I wanted was Him. I dreamed of the days gone by when I felt so close to Him and His peace was always with me. I remembered what His peace felt like from when I was much younger and I knew I could never settle for anything less in my relationship with Jesus. I was determined to find that deep peace again. I was so desperate for God to deliver me from all of my suffering. Jesus was the only way out of this bottomless pit I was in.

It was in that pit that I sought after God like I had never before. Before this, I lived for me. It was all about what I could get, making sure I was having a good time, having more to drink, getting more attention, more affection and flattery, more emotional connections, and more sexual connections. My agenda before this was all about living it up, until my very life was nearly stripped from me. What seemed so important before this dark night season looked like garbage now. It literally meant nothing to me. Living my life as a lesbian was incomprehensible. Drinking and partying were no longer a desire for me. All

I cared about was being right with God. Like Saul's conversion before he became Paul, I was awakened in my blindness.[27]

Life Preserver

This transformational season of my life was particularly difficult. I moved back home in July of 2007 because I needed my family around me for support. In October of 2007, God showed me a picture or vision of myself drowning in an ocean. The waves were crashing in on me, and I was drowning. I could not breathe or stay afloat any longer. I had been in this sea of despair and darkness for so long that I was simply exhausted. I saw a woman on a large ship, and she noticed me drowning. She threw a life preserver out to me to save me. As I reached to grab a hold of the float, she started reeling me in by a rope that was attached to it. She pulled me onto the ship, into safety. This vision truly gave me the hope that a special Good Samaritan was on the way.

I was so low at this point that I knew I needed counseling. My mom had a counselor named Jamie she trusted, so I decided to meet with her. Jamie counseled me and shared with me. She told me about a healing/deliverance ministry team she was a part of. She told me all about

Hope For Freedom

their ministry and offered to take me to meet with her leader, Pastor Johnson. Shortly thereafter, I met with Pastor Johnson and she presented me with a hope that I needed so desperately. She was the lady I envisioned on the ship. She loved me with the love of Jesus and took me in under her wing like a momma eagle. She believed in me and would not let me go until I was safe with Jesus. God sent her to me to bring me back to life. She was my Good Samaritan.

Vision of Healing

In our sessions, I explained to her that the last two years of my life were hell, that I had lost almost all hope, and that I was scared that no one was ever going to hear my cry for help. Pastor Johnson did what no one else would do. Rather than pass me by because the help I needed was too difficult, she stepped into the middle of my mess with me and became deeply involved in my healing and deliverance.

As Pastor Johnson ministered to me, it was Jesus who poured the balm of healing oil over my deepest wounds to soothe my pain. He poured His blood into my wounds to bring forgiveness and healing.[28] Last of all, He covered my wounds through His love, to prevent infection from worsening my condition. The devil wanted to leave all my wounds exposed and vulnerable to allow for continued relapses into sin. Psalm 147:3 says that Jesus *"...heals the brokenhearted and binds up their wounds."*[29] I was in so much pain that I didn't realize it was Jesus carrying me until after I had recovered. I received inner healing from her prayer ministry for just over one year. I knew that if God had brought me this far in my healing journey, He would carry me to the finish line.

Before my time of healing with Pastor Johnson, I couldn't trust anyone. I was closed inside. My heart was hardened and I didn't want people to see me or my brokenness. After meeting with Pastor Johnson, I started to believe in God's people again. It started little by little with opening up and letting people in again. Before this, I was like a wounded animal, hurt and trapped in a snare. I was scared to death for anyone to get close because it was just too painful. I wanted to "self-protect." After all, that's how I had survived up to this point, so I thought.

Through this healing, I finally let go of the fear of rejection and judgement, and started trusting. After long hours of prayer with Pastor Johnson and her team, I stopped wrestling and fighting them long enough for Jesus to come in to my deepest pain.

This healing journey made me reflect on a time back in 2006 when I was driving around in my car, crying out to God from the depths of my soul saying, "Why God?! You can heal me in a second, Father, a minute, a day?! Why can't you and why won't you heal me? Take this pain from me. I know you can. I believe you can. I beg you, Father, show me why?!" I was crying so hard I had to pull over. There I was, sitting on the side of the highway in my car doubled over on my steering wheel.

That day, Father God showed His tenderness toward me and my pain. He assured me of His concern and care for every single wound. I realized then that my healing journey would be a process. He was with me and He wasn't going to leave me in that wounded condition. God gave me a vision to help me understand His plan for my healing:

> *I could see me as a 3- or 4-year-old, and I was playing outside at my parents' house where I grew up. I went out in the backyard and I fell into a briar patch. The thorn bush I fell into was big and I could*

see myself lying there. I was stuck. I couldn't move from the unbearable pain of the thorns. The big thorns covered my whole body from head to toe. I remember feeling helpless. I looked around and no one was there. I was afraid.

Suddenly, my father came running to me and knelt beside me. (In my vision my earthly father represented my Heavenly Father.) He looked at me and gently smiled. He was concerned for me. He said, "Dana, I can only delicately and gently pull one thorn out at a time. The pain would be unbearable if I started pulling all of them out at once."

Breaking off Lies

I distinctly remember another vision that Michael, one of the prayer partners, had during my time with Pastor Johnson and team:

He saw a long hallway with many rooms to the left and right. As Pastor Johnson and her healing team would go into each room (my heart), Jesus would come in with them

109

*and when they left a room, Jesus would
sweep it clean, lock and seal the door.*

Jesus came into every room of my heart and did some
deep cleaning. He was breaking off lie after lie with His
love and truth. The lies were like a big ball of yarn that
was all tangled and knotted together. The idea of
untangling this ball of lies on my own was overwhelming
to think about and felt impossible. The lies the enemy
was telling me were not uncommon, but I still had to
remember what the Bible said about each and every one
of those lies. Here are some examples:

The enemy says, "You're going to die."

The Bible says, *"I shall not die, but live, and declare the
works of the Lord."*[30]

The enemy says, "You'll never make it."

The Bible says, *"And I am sure of this, that He who began
a good work in you will bring it to completion."*[31]

The enemy says, "You'll never be free."

The Bible says, *"So if the son sets you free, you will be
free indeed."*[32]

The enemy says, "You are too far gone."

The Bible says, *"If we acknowledge our sins, he is faithful and just and will forgive our* sins and cleanse us from every wrongdoing."*33*

The enemy says, "You'll lose your mind."

The Bible says, *"For God has not given us a spirit of fear and timidity, but of power, love and a sound mind."34*

The enemy says, "You are damaged merchandise."

The Bible says, *"He is before all things, and in Him all things hold together."35*

The enemy says, "You are never going to be good enough."

The Bible says, *"To the one who is able to keep you from stumbling and to present you unblemished and exultant, in the presence of his glory."36*

The enemy says, "You blew it. You will never be whole."

The Bible says, *"He who was seated on the throne said, "I am making all things new!"37*

The enemy of our soul wants us as his slave. He wants to hold us in bondage in our minds. It all starts in our mind and our way of thinking. If I believed I was not good enough, I would constantly strive to measure up feeling like I never could. If I believed that I was born gay, then I would live a gay lifestyle. If I believed I was the "wrong gender" or that God made a mistake, I would live like the opposite sex, possibly even going so far as to have surgery for a gender reassignment.

The enemy bombarded me with so many lies all at one time. The web was so tangled, that I couldn't remember what the truth really was. I had so much confusion and fogginess, which I know does not come from God. I believed the lie that God had abandoned me. The enemy had convinced me I was too far gone, that I could never be whole again.

At one point, I believed my lot in life was to be identified as a lesbian, and that was just how it was going to be. I couldn't see a way out, and quite frankly I didn't want out because the lies were easier to believe. I settled for what these lies said to be true of me. I believed I had failed God so many times that He let me go. I believed there was no way back and that I couldn't return to God again because of all those failures. If I ever did try to return, I was terrified I would just fail Him again like I did all those times before.

This bondage of lies began in my mind. I was so deceived I believed that I was going to die or end up in a mental institution. I believed there was no hope for me. I was not grounded in God's word, which would have reminded me of the truth and allowed me to differentiate the lies from reality. The enemy targets all our weak spots. He knew I had many wrong mindsets and mental strongholds that had been built up over the years.

The enemy wanted to destroy me. He wanted to halt God's divine purpose in my life. He had no mercy for me, one of God's children. How did he do that? He started by planting lies in the form of seeds of doubt, confusion and deception in my mind. Because I was unaware those thoughts were lies from the enemy, the seeds had plenty of room to build a fortress of lies with a firm foundation. This started when I was very young. The lies led to wrong mindsets and mental strongholds. The mindsets caused me to come in to agreement with the enemy's lies. Once I agreed, the demonic thoughts began to poison my mind and the lies became my reality.

I know now that whatever we believe in our mind, whether good or bad, truth or lies, will become our reality. We are what we think, and we must be intentional about what we're thinking about. We have to purposefully decide to be like-minded with God, and choose right thoughts. It is a process. How do we know if a thought is a lie from the enemy or the truth from God? The truth is always revealed through God's word, the Bible, but sadly, people don't always accept it. Joyce Meyer says, "Our carnal (worldly, fleshy) minds have had so much practice operating freely that we surely don't have to use any effort to think wrong thoughts."[38]

We must know God's word in order to choose the truth. In Psalm 119:11, David said, *"I have hidden your word in my heart that I might not sin against you."[39]* This isn't just God's list of do's and don'ts, it is also His truths about us and who we are in Him. The Bible reminds us that Jesus is the way, the truth, and the life. We can know the truth when we know Jesus personally. We must choose to align our thoughts with the thoughts of Jesus, the mind of Christ. When we recognize a thought is a lie, we have to replace it with the truth, the Word of God.

We have a responsibility, as children of God, to choose holy and true thoughts. Our mind has to be renewed daily by God's Word in order to follow after the Spirit and not the flesh. Philippians 4:8 says, *"Finally brothers and sisters, whatever is true, whatever is noble, whatever is right, whatever is pure, whatever is lovely, whatever is admirable - if anything is excellent or praiseworthy - think about such things."*[40] When a negative or sexual thought pops in my head, I have a choice in how to respond. I can agree with, entertain or fantasize about it, or reject and replace that thought with the truth found in the Bible. It takes practice, and it certainly takes time.

Joyce Meyer has also said, "Think about what you're thinking about." [41] We must be intentional in our thinking. We need to be aware of and prudent in our attitudes and in our thought life. What are you thinking about? Matthew 15:18 says, *"But the things that come out of a person's mouth come from the heart, and these defile them."* [42] Whatever you think and believe about yourself will come out in some way, so be vigilant in breaking off the lies.

Freedom Firsts

Not only did God need to break off lies to restore me, but also the lies in my family to bring healing and restoration to them. I was blessed that my parents were so involved in this journey with me. Because of that, I experienced a level of deep healing with my mom and dad. Throughout my lesbian life, the enemy drove a wedge between my parents and I to steal our trust, love and understanding we had with each other. The enemy used lies, unforgiveness, mistrust, bitterness, and resentfulness in the attempt to destroy my relationship with my parents.

One day in our prayer sessions, my parents and I were able to sit down together and have an open conversation. Jesus met us there and came into some deep places of hurt, pain and unforgiveness in all of us. In humility, I could see and admit my wrongs and see the pain I had caused them. I was sincerely sorry for it all. Likewise, my parents came to a place where they could acknowledge and take responsibility for the ways they didn't respond to me with understanding and unconditional love at times (especially while I was living in the lesbian lifestyle).

I was so grateful to openly share with my parents the deep pains from my childhood, all of the losses while living in the lesbian lifestyle, especially Lori. My mom held me and we both wept together. She was finally open to see and feel my deepest pain for the first time. I needed her to acknowledge my pain and loss of Lori. It was like a death to me. I needed her to know it was real. I needed my parents to know the struggle I endured all those years in the lifestyle.

Our family healing is still a work in progress. This work takes openness, unconditional love, humility, understanding, admitting wrongs, forgiveness, an open heart and Jesus' mercy. Jesus is in the business of restoring what was lost in our hearts and in our families. All we lost was found through Jesus. Colossians 1:17 says, *"He is before all things, and in Him all things hold together."*[43] Jesus' love holds all things together. Jesus picks up all the broken pieces of our hearts and puts them back together again. Jesus wants and can make all things new. Revelation 21:5 says, *"And He who was seated on the throne said, 'Behold, I am making all things new.'"*[44]

Even though we were making a lot of progress in our family prayer sessions, there was still a fear in my dad's heart manifesting as a lie. In one session, Pastor Johnson looked into my dad's eyes and said firmly, "She's not going back, Rip! Dana's not going back into the lesbian lifestyle. It is finished. The enemy wants you to believe and come into agreement with the lie that says, 'Dana will go back... and doubt what God has done in her heart.'"

I could feel the power of the lie break when Pastor Johnson spoke that out loud to him. I knew it was finished. God had delivered me. I had learned the lesson.

Through my consequences, I had learned obedience was better than sacrifice. It was through the darkness that I could see the light...the truth. Hebrews 5:8 says, *"Son though He was, He learned obedience from the things He suffered."*[45]

At this point, I could see the choices I had made for my life didn't only affect me, my salvation and relationship with God, it also had an emotional and spiritual impact on my whole family. My decisions gravely impacted my entire family, friends and the body of Christ as a whole. My sin damaged and hurt my brother, sister, and obviously, my mom and dad. Sin, in any form, leaves its mark on those that are closest to us. Sin wounds our soul and damages the ones we love the most. Sin separates. It divides our hearts from God and from one another. The enemy's largest target is the family. He wants to separate and divide everyone and everything.

I wasn't going to let that happen to me or my family anymore. After the year I spent in prayer with Pastor Johnson and her team, I came into a place of freedom. It was not only amazing but also peaceful and sweet. There was rejoicing and I even had joy again. Our family finally could laugh again. Psalm 30:5 says, *"Weeping may stay for the night, but rejoicing comes in the morning."*[46]

It was like a dream for me. I started sleeping normally again. I started to dance, sing and shout again. I had hope again. I experienced major breakthroughs in many areas of my life. It didn't happen overnight, but God was working behind the scenes. It was a process. He made a way for me where there seemed to be no way out. He is my "Mighty Deliverer." He heard my cry from the depths of my soul and He came to my rescue. He is my rock. Psalm 18:2 says, *"The Lord is my rock, my fortress and my deliverer; my God is my rock, in whom I take refuge, my shield and the horn of my salvation, my stronghold."*[47]

7

Hindsight is 20/20

"True, God is our Heavenly Father, and He dearly loves us; however He seeks our best interest, which is not always what we want, what satisfies for the moment, or what makes us happy in this instant."[48] -Trevor Bowen

Sting of Sin

Sirach 15:16-17 says, *"There are set before you fire and water; to whichever you choose, stretch forth your hand. Before men are life and death, whichever he chooses shall be given him."*[49]

During my dark night season, I was driving my car and I remember feeling stripped of my very life. I was in what felt like the deepest pit and I begged God to reveal Himself to me. I just needed to know that He was with me because it felt like I was holding on by one single thread. I had to pull over on the side of the road because I was crying so hard. As I was crying out to God, I didn't necessarily feel His presence in a tangible way, but He did give me a vision or picture of what had happened to me with regards to the dark night. I was so thankful that

I could come to Him like David did in Psalm 34:4, *"I sought the Lord, and he answered me."*[50]

In this vision, I was about 4 years old. I saw a kitchen and it had a huge pot of boiling water on the stove. This pot was the size of a massive crawfish pot. The water in the pot was almost boiling over. I made my way towards the pot, and as I was stretching my hand to grab it, Father God gently tapped my little hand and told me, "No, Dana." He then gently turned me completely opposite from where the boiling water was and guided me away from it.

I saw this scenario happen repeatedly. Time and time again Father God would lovingly and gently tell me, "No, Dana. It's going to hurt you. Let me show you another way. I have a better way for you." Yet I would continue to go back to that same pot of boiling water over and over again. The last time I went back to the pot of boiling water I got a hold of it, pulled it over onto me, and my whole body was severely burned.

This vision helped me to see and understand why God had allowed me to go through that experience. After receiving this clear vision, it was still difficult to put into words all that God spoke to me through it. At first, I was without words and the tears just fell. God revealed to me exactly what I had asked Him for.

Obviously, the pot of boiling water represented the sin that I repeatedly went back to. The Lord gave me countless warnings and ways to avoid this tragedy from taking place. I know now that if I had heeded the warnings that God had given me, I would not have gone through most of this. God, like a patient and loving parent, gently slapped my hand over and over again hoping it would be enough to keep me out of the danger I was headed towards. He tried to direct me and guide me so many times throughout my life. He could see the big picture and knew what was best for me.

All those warnings were not enough to change my mind. The gift of free will was a double-edged sword for me. I had a choice to continue to go my own way or heed God's warnings and follow Him. He was only able to do as much as He could to protect me. Just like all parents, God finally let me make my own decision and experience the consequences.

I didn't know or understand all of the consequences that I would endure by not heeding God's warnings. Looking back, it would have been better to heed them, rather than having to go through the dark night. It would have been better to get out of the lesbian lifestyle sooner rather than get burned repeatedly. It would have been better to respond to God's mercy rather than have to go through the chastening of the Lord, brought on by my poor choices.

I've shared how God warned me through dreams and visions but because I had this stubborn and prideful attitude of heart, I didn't want His help. One example of God's gracious and persistent attempts at intervention was one night when I went to a local bar to drink and shoot pool with a friend. It was a small local bar and everyone knew everyone else's name. I was in a pool game when I noticed an unfamiliar man who walked in and stood at the corner of the bar. He was middle aged and had dark hair.

Not long after he arrived, he proceeded to walk directly up to me at my table. He seemed very intentional.

The man stared right through me and asked, "Do you know who I am?"

I said, "No, sir."

He said, "My name is Michael. You know you don't belong here."

He never stopped staring and I could feel that we connected in the Spirit of God.

Sternly, he said, "You know you don't belong here."

I was speechless. His words struck me to my core. Before I could blink my eye, the man was gone. There was no trace of him after that encounter. I left my pool game and ice cold beer sitting there and I took off instantly. At that moment, my heart felt God's merciful conviction of my lifestyle yet again. I believe the man in the bar that night was Michael, the Archangel, sent by God to warn me.

The Dog Returns to His Vomit

Proverbs 26:11 *"As a dog returns to his vomit, so a fool repeats his folly.*[51]

The author of Proverbs was indicating the fool is stuck in their way of thinking, or choices, by repeating the same mistake over and over again. The question I asked myself was, "Why did I keep going back?" What makes a dog return to its vomit? If you've ever seen a dog do this, it is almost as if it is compelled by some force or instinct to return.

We humans do the same thing sometimes. As Peter said in 2 Peter 2:12, *"They are like unreasoning animals, creatures of **instinct**, ...and like animals, they too will perish."*[52] I felt like an animal acting out of compulsion. I felt like I had no control. It was as if my flesh was chanting, "I must feed my emotional, alcohol, and sexual addictions."

I kept going back because I was stuck in my way of thinking. I had mental strongholds that I had allowed the enemy to build that convinced me of many things that were not the truth about me. I believed the devil's lies and lived in deception. I believed I was born a lesbian and the lifestyle was probably the best I could expect from life. I believed this was all I deserved, and this was my lot here on earth. I settled for less. All the while, God had a better way for me. He had life, and not just life, but life in abundance![53]

God had a spiritual feast waiting for me at His banquet table. While in the lesbian lifestyle, I had settled for a smaller and more pain-filled life than what God had created for me. It was like eating crumbs that fell of the table or scraps out of a garbage dump in comparison to living in full communion with God and feasting at His table. I settled for what taking the path of least resistance presented me with, not believing that God had a better plan for me.

When all you know are crumbs and scraps, they seem good enough. They are not that bad when you are really hungry. You can live on scraps and crumbs your whole life and be satisfied if that's all you've ever known. But once you've eaten from a banquet table, and feasted on fine foods, the scraps and crumbs would never get a second glance. My lot in life was not to live as a lesbian. My identity was not being a lesbian.

Looking back, I see the abundance that God had waiting for me all along. He watched and waited for me to come home. He couldn't wait to put His robe of righteousness on me, to put His ring on my finger, and slaughter the fattened calf on behalf of my return to Him.[54] Oh, what a feast the Lord Jesus set before me! I feast on His love and mercy while my enemies watch. I am so grateful to eat at the Lord's table. It is as sweet as honey from the honeycomb.

Stop of the Cycle of Addiction

As an addict, how do you stop returning to your addictions? I have pondered this question in my heart for a long time. If anyone who suffers from any addiction wants to be free from it, it is very difficult to nearly impossible to break the addiction with your own good intentions, merits, or strong will. Although those ambitions might be a good start, even getting you "free" for a season, it's difficult to maintain alone.

Every addiction is a means of filling a void or emptiness in us. It's a way we cope or survive we have become accustomed or familiar with. Most addictions are a quick-fix for a deeper need or longing than what the addiction appears to address on the surface.

Addictions are outward symptoms or manifestations of what is lacking or broken inside. Until we allow Jesus to get to the root of our pain and brokenness, we will always desire that fix that satisfies for the moment while leaving us even more empty after we indulge.

Albert Einstein said, "The definition of insanity is doing the same thing over and over again, but expecting different results." In our efforts to overcome addictions in our lives, there must come a time when we decide to break the cycle and do something different than what we have always done. It was a long journey, but I'm thankful I finally reached that point and chose Jesus.

Jesus Christ is the ultimate rope of hope. He is the way to freedom and staying free from our addictions. Ultimately, it's the blood that Jesus willingly shed that breaks, looses, cuts and dissolves all strongholds in our lives.

Addictions and bad habits don't go away overnight. It is a process, sometimes a long process. In our best efforts, we may fall at times, but we must continuously maintain the heart-posture of being made complete in Jesus. We must want Jesus more than anything else. We must lay our lives down completely, not holding anything back. It is all or nothing, if you want to live in freedom from addiction. In dying to ourselves and our short-sighted desires, we are able to live in freedom and victory through Jesus.

We also need the body of Christ to help us heal from our addictions and sins as well. We need to hold ourselves accountable to God first, then we need accountability with a respected authority from the body of Christ. We were not designed to do life alone, like someone isolated on an island. We were made for community. Through the body of Christ, we can be more complete and be who God has made us to be.

Jude says people stay in this state of addiction because they "do not have the Spirit."[55] The Holy Spirit gives us wisdom and revelation to choose life in abundance. Life or death would seem to be an obvious choice but evidently it is a difficult one we still need some help making. Deuteronomy 30:19 says, *"Today, I have given you the choice between life and death, blessings or curses. Now choose life, so that you and your children may live."*[56]

The options of life and death are set before us and it is our choice. There is no neutral or gray area. Like it or not, you possess a free will and have the responsibility of deciding. There's God and life in abundance, or the enemy and death. The choices you make today, whether large or small, will determine your future and ultimately your eternity.

Taking God for Granted

"Grace is akin to the extra time an individual gets to live after the doctors have shortened it in their estimation; grace is the brief moment the sun pushes the storm clouds aside on a gloomy day. Grace is quite possibly the most beautiful also the most abused gift that Jesus gave to us."[57]*-Anissa Rowe*

As I look back, I learned that I took God's love and mercy for granted. I abused God's grace. I presumed, in my arrogance, that I could continue living out of God's holy design, and therefore escape any consequences for the poor decisions I made for my life. Every decision, big or small, good or bad, had consequences. I can see clearly now how easily I was deceived in my thinking. I had a spirit of presumption and a haughty attitude toward God and His ways. However, I am now passionate, sharing from my experience, a warning to those who are living their own way in pride and self-sufficiency.

There are two scriptures the Lord revealed to me about presumption. The first scripture is James 4:13-16. It says, *"Come now, you who say, 'Today or tomorrow we will go into such and such a city, and spend a year there and engage in business and make a profit.' Yet you do not know what your life will be like tomorrow. You are just a vapor that appears for a little while and then vanishes away. Instead, you ought to say, 'If the Lord wills, we will live and also do this or that.' But as it is you boast in your arrogance; all such boasting is evil."*[58]

In refection, I look back and clearly see how I assumed that my life was something that I could control. I did what I wanted, when I wanted. I never thought there would be any consequences for my rebellious living. I wasn't concerned for the poor, the broken, or the people in prison. Heck, I was living in my own prison in my self-centered life. I was blind to the fact that life is short, and God made me for His purpose, to serve and love His people. I was so into myself and material possessions that I never saw anyone else's needs besides my own.

I assumed I had all the time in the world, so I put God off. It started day to day, month to month, and then year to year. That year of putting God off soon became a decade. I placed God and His will for my life on the back burner and went about living like I had all the time in the world.

The second scripture the Lord led me to is Sirach 5:6. This scripture speaks of pride, independence, and false security. It says *"Of forgiveness be not overconfident, adding sin upon sin. Say not: Great is His mercy; my many sins He will forgive."*[59]

While living as a prodigal, I abused God's grace by adding sin upon sin. Yes, God forgives every time. Romans 6:1 says, *"What then shall we say? Shall we persist in sin that grace may abound? Of course not!"*[60] I was convicted and was truly sorry. I realized the longer I stayed in the lifestyle, the larger my heart attitude of deep-rooted rebellion and pride grew. I didn't want to change. I didn't want to let go of my sin.

Because I let this attitude take over for a while, it caused me to have a numbed conscience for what grieved God's heart. I strayed so far away from God I couldn't see my need for Him anymore. I lost my sensitivity to the Lord's tender love in my heart by my own doing.

I called on God when I needed something. I selfishly believed that I could have His peace whenever I wanted it, even though I was living in complete disobedience. I still acknowledged my belief in Jesus, and all it entailed, but to be able to continue living in sin, I kept God at a distance. I took His love for granted and decided I could live outside of His design for me and never have consequences for the choices I made.

My actions were like a spoiled child who wanted all the benefits given to me by my parents, but without honoring or valuing them. My love was immature. I loved when it was convenient and fulfilled my desires. I loved Jesus so much yet still lacked commitment and loyalty.

In the midst of my dark night season, Father God showed me a vision while in prayer. He showed me a bridge in our hometown. In my vision, the bridge was fractured and almost completely severed in the middle yet miraculously still connected. The coils and the concrete from the bridge's foundation were all dismantled and some parts were hanging off the bridge. This bridge had surely taken a beating.

I realized the bridge was broken on my end because I was the unfaithful one. The bridge in my vision helped me visualize the damage that was done in my relationship with Father God. We shared an intimate relationship where trust and love were built and strengthened by our commitment of fidelity to one another. It's like a marriage because I am part of the bride of Christ.

I needed to choose faithfulness and obedience to reconcile our relationship. There were times in my prayer life when it was so difficult to feel connected with Father God. I was specifically praying about feeling disconnected with Him when God spoke to me and said, "It takes time to rebuild trust that has been broken."

Chastening

Hebrews 12:11 *"Now no chastening seems to be joyful for the present, but painful; nevertheless, afterward it yields the peaceable fruit of righteousness to those who have been trained by it."*[61]

134

After sharing some of my story several years ago with a dear friend, she said, "Dana you were so far from home that I think God had to spank you all the way back home!"

Proverbs 3:12 says, *"For the Lord disciplines those He loves, just as a father corrects a child in whom He delights in."*[62]

When I first heard this saying from that friend, I didn't like it. It seemed so harsh and cruel. I thought to myself, "God wouldn't spank me or would He?" Was I being severely disciplined by God? I didn't comprehend the loving aspect of the reproof of the Lord because at the time, it was too painful to believe. Although now I have come to realize that there was profound truth and wisdom in what she said.

Through the dark night season, it was too difficult for me to understand what was happening and why it was happening. I know now it definitely was a chastening from the Lord. I didn't see it through the perspective of the love of the Father while it was going on. Now, I can see it all through the lens of love of my heavenly Father and it has brought me to a deep place of humility.

It has helped me see and know how much He really, really loves me. I was so thankful for His long-suffering.

God has also shown me the difference between a healthy fear of the Lord versus an unhealthy one. It transformed the spoiled child into a grateful, obedient, and loving child.

Our Father knows the big picture He designed for our lives. He knows what's going to hurt or destroy us. He wants to protect us from danger because He is truly our Good Shepherd. When God chastens us, it marks us. It's like a calf being branded by its owner. First, we are marked by the seal of His love. 2 Corinthians 1:22 says, *"He has set his seal of ownership on us, and put his Spirit in our hearts as a deposit, guaranteeing what is to come."*[63]

When a farmer brands his livestock, it's a memorable occasion for the calf. It is branded for life. If the calf is stolen or lost, it can be identified and returned to its owner because bears the brand. It was for my benefit and safety that the Lord chastised me. I learned obedience through the pain of correction. Hebrews 5:8 says, *"Son though He was, he learned obedience from what he suffered."*[64]

If Jesus Christ had to learn obedience through His suffering, then how can I possibly escape learning obedience from my suffering? Author Bob Sorge has said, "Chastening is a mark of son-ship. It means that the son/daughter is loved and the father is engaged and caring. The only reason a loving (earthly) father wouldn't chasten his son is if he is jaded against its wisdom."[65]

Today, if I get close to that pot of boiling water, I remember its sting. I can recall with immense clarity the smell, taste and feel the burn gave me. The chastening of the Lord was a gift. I was allowed to taste death without dying. I was privileged to experience the goodness and mercy of God in a way that I have never before, as well as the sweet redemption of my pain.

During the dark night season, I spent some time in the Adoration Chapel one day and I was kneeling before the Lord. As I was praying regarding the pain I was in, I had a vision. I could see red roses at Jesus' feet. Every time I would release my pain and suffering up to Him, another red rose was added to the pile at His feet. Before I knew it, the pile of roses was so high and enormous I couldn't see Jesus anymore. The pile of red roses was high over His head. Jesus said to me, "My little one, your suffering will not be in vain. It is a fragrant aroma to me." 2 Corinthians 2:15 says, *"For we are to God the pleasing aroma of Christ among those who are being saved and those who are perishing.*[66]

I know I never want to go back into the lesbian lifestyle. I don't want to. I'm not saying I will never have temptation. I do have temptation. Jesus was tempted in the desert. Everyone who walks this earth will be tempted. That place of darkness is a place that I will never forget. It's marked me. It's branded me for life.

Deuteronomy 8:5 says, *"Thus you are to know in your heart that the Lord your God was disciplining you just as a man disciplines His son."*[67]

I delight in obedience to God now. I want to stay as far away from sin as I can, and I know it's only by the grace of God I can live in that freedom. God revealed to me sin in any form leads to danger and eventually death. Sin is ugly and vile in all its form. My dad loves to say, "You can't keep going back to the pig pen and expect not to get dirty." Sin gets us dirty, filthy, and it separates us from the Father. God hates sin but He loves the sinner. He loves us in spite of our sin and that's why Jesus died for us. We wouldn't need a savior if we were all perfect.

"In the book of Hosea, Gomer, the adulteress, symbolized faithless Israel."[68] And just as Hosea could not give up his wife forever, even when she played the harlot, so Yahweh could not renounce Israel, who was betrothed to him. God chastised them in order to bring back His beloved to the fresh and pure joy of their first love. Israel's infidelity took the form of idolatry and ruthless oppression of the poor. No amount of mechanically offered sacrifices could atone for her serious sins.

"Chastisement alone remained; God would have to strip her of the rich ornaments bestowed by her false lovers and thus bring her back to Him. A humiliated Israel would again seek Yahweh. Hosea 11 is one of the summits of Old Testament theology; God's love for His people has never been expressed more tenderly."[69]

I was like Gomer, the adulteress. I kept going back to my false lovers. In God's relentless love for me, he had to correct my disobedience. He had to chastise me, but it was out of His longing to bring me back to the pure joy of my first love. After being stripped of all the remnants of my infidelity, I was brought to a humble place before God.

He never gave up on me, even when I turned my back on him. When I was faithless, He remained faithful. He stays committed and continuously pursues us. His relentless love and mercy has humbled me and I am so grateful for it.

8

The Great Exchange

"God reconciled sinful man to Himself by making His sinless son the sin-bearer and dying in the sinner's place. Jesus Christ paid the death penalty for the sinner, so that God could set the sinner free and declare him righteous in His holy presence. Moreover, he did more than just forgive us our sins; He imputed the perfect righteousness of his son to us. A great exchange took place. Christ got all our sin and guilt; we got His perfect righteousness standing before God. His righteousness is exchanged for our sin."
-Wil Pounds

Determined to Get to the Healer

Several years ago, I was listening to a Nigerian priest preach. He was sharing from Luke 8:43, about the story of the woman who had been bleeding for twelve years coming through the crowd to touch Jesus' tassel and the active pursuit that healed her. As he was preaching, I could see myself in this woman, lost in the crowd, unable to see my way to Jesus, much less get to Him. I could feel the crowd pushing in on me, slowing me down with their resistance. I was reaching and fighting my way through but was still tossed to and fro. I couldn't find Jesus. There were too many people positioned as obstacles in my way. I was determined to get to Jesus.

There were so many people in my way and I could feel the struggle. I thought to myself, trying to get through on my feet isn't working. So, what if I crawl? I fell to my hands and knees and started crawling. I instantly became grimy, muddy and filthy from the dirty streets. It was painful fighting through all the people. They were stepping all over me. Like this woman that was bleeding and so desperate for Jesus' healing touch, I too was desperate and determined to get to Jesus. I knew if I could get to Him, He would heal me...completely. I knew He could heal my broken heart, my alcohol addiction, my sexual and emotional addiction to women, my fears, my fear of man, and my distorted desires.

I was also keenly aware that this was a battle to get to Jesus. It was a fight to get through the people. I had to get past their opinions of me, my broken past, my lesbian identity and lifestyle, all my addictions, even the harsh and critical judgments from friends who didn't understand my conversion. I had to fight my way out of all of it.

God was showing me that this was a battle I couldn't win on my own. God's grace was what would get me past all the resistance. This was the beginning of my healing process. This was the beginning of my great exchange.

New Creation

"Therefore, if anyone is in Christ, the old has passed away; behold the new has come." 2 Corinthians 5:17[70]

Several years ago, God showed me an image while praying with a friend of mine. She was experiencing instability in her heart from childhood abuse. The image I saw while praying with her was an old white house, tattered and broken on the outside. This house was literally falling apart. This house seemed to be a perfect candidate for complete demolition. Inside the house were cracked floors, and in some rooms, the floors were caving in. It was dark throughout most of the house. Suddenly, a big crane with a wrecking ball on it began tearing it down.

As I continued to pray for her, I sensed that Jesus was breaking off lies that she believed from her childhood. He was demolishing the old house which represented her old belief system, so He could build a brand new one, It was to be a new creation or a new dwelling for Him to

143

live in. For if we are Christians, we are filled with the Holy Spirit and God makes His home in our hearts.

I discovered that I am a living temple, or home for God. 1 Corinthians 6:19 says, *"Don't you realize that your body is the temple of the Holy Spirit, who lives in you and was given to you by God? You do not belong to yourself."[71]* Through my healing journey, I have discovered that I had serious foundational issues in my spiritual house from my childhood.

Why does God demolish the old for the new?

Throughout my healing process, I felt God's wrecking ball. He worked to tear down the lies I was hiding behind. He revealed some deep roots of rejection that had taken hold of me, and caused me to have fractures in my foundation as a child. He unveiled many gaps in bonding or connecting emotionally with my mom, dad and sister early on which caused me to feel not good enough and rejected. He continues to replace every lie with His truth. The truth and healing with my family has been exponential in these last few years. God has exchanged my rejection for His acceptance.

I had also been hiding behind my identity as a lesbian. My lesbian identity made me feel unstoppable, tough and powerful. It was a facade and a false sense of identity and security. In reality, I was insecure, weak and powerless. God started gently highlighting the areas of my brokenness in the ways I would self-protect me. God exchanged my false identity with a true and authentic identity in Him.

God gently exposed some deep foundational cracks regarding trusting boys and men in my childhood. I perceived myself as weak because of the verbal and sexual abuse in my early years. I set up many barriers and walls that guarded my heart against intimacy and trust with men. That guard was so stealthy that I wasn't even aware of my fear of intimacy with men until several years ago. I would only allow men to get so close before pushing them away.

In my past, I thought if I could look and act tough enough, I would not be vulnerable with men. Identifying as a lesbian was an easy way to self-protect and avoid having any kind of intimacy with a man. I mistakenly thought I was protecting myself which was an illusion. It was deception and caused more damage than protection. Jesus is my ultimate protector and I rest in that. God exchanged my fear of men for a heart that could trust men again.

Another exchange was when I relinquished control of protecting myself and allowed Jesus to be in charge of caring for me. I trust in His leadership and believe He will give me my hearts' desire in His perfect timing (like a man who loves Jesus as much as I do and beautiful children, too.)

Being Vulnerable with Jesus

God is continually calling me to lay down my tough girl protective gear and lay bare before Him. God revealed a vision to a friend of mine as she was praying for me a few years ago. She saw two pictures of me, the first image she saw was of me wearing this tough medieval armor with spikes on the elbows, knees, helmet, basically the whole armor. The second image she saw was of me lying prostrate at Jesus' feet, barefoot with shorts and a t-shirt.

Then she saw the armored me ride up on a motorcycle looking at the t-shirt and shorts version of me lying on my face before Him. As tough me looked at vulnerable me, tough me said to my friend, "You mean I have to take this armor off, too?" As my friend shared this image with me, I just broke. God was inviting me to lay it down. I wanted to lay down all the heavy protective gear I had been wearing for years. I was so tired. It was a burden but it was the only safety I knew.

I knew I had to let go and take off my tough girl armor, allowing myself to be undone before Him. There are still times when I realize I have placed my tough girl armor on again. I continue to trust Jesus knowing I am safe in Him. The great exchange is being vulnerable with Jesus, saying, "I can't do this on my own."

I have also been able to embrace my beautiful feminine self. For so long, I suppressed my feminine side. Living as a lesbian, I suppressed anything that felt weak. God has unveiled my feminine beauty that had been hidden within.

God exchanged my tough girl image into a beautiful, vulnerable, feminine woman. Now, don't get me wrong. I still like sports, getting muddy, wearing hoodies and riding on four wheelers. God hasn't taken away who He has made me to be, He is simply revealing my true feminine self. I feel I am blooming like a flower. God is opening the beautiful woman He created me to be and it feels amazing. I even enjoy wearing dresses for special occasions now and feel very beautiful in them. Which is a long way from before where I felt awkward and uncomfortable in anything girly. Living in His truth, I can accept me as a beautiful woman and live in that freedom.

Beyond Brokenness

"Other people are going to find healing in your wounds. Your greatest life messages and your most effective ministry will come out of your deepest hurts."[72] *-Rick Warren*

For so many years, I wanted to hide the broken pieces of my heart and life. I did a good job at it, I thought. I didn't want anyone to see how broken I was and possibly reject me even further. There is something about us as human beings always wanting to look like we have it all together.

My healing of PTSD has been a very slow, ongoing, and challenging process, to say the least. It has affected every area of my life. It's not like an injury that you can tangibly put your finger on, like that of a broken leg. PTSD is an invisible wound. "It was like I was shot with an invisible bullet and bled invisible blood."[73] The emotional and physiological damage done was like an earthquake. It shook me to my core, and left a wake of destruction. The aftershocks are still very agonizing at times.

I was so broken I felt I had nothing to give to my family, friends or church. I felt incompetent. I felt useless when I was experiencing the severe effects of PTSD and it translated into shame and disgrace. I felt I was damaged merchandise left under the rubble of an earthquake.

Previously, I was the kind of person who would just pull myself up by the boot straps and do what needed to be done no matter what. I could handle anything that came my way. I had always had a positive outlook on life and always saw the good even in the worst of situations.

This psychological limp that I've walked with reminds me of Paul's thorn in the flesh. Like Paul, I don't understand it, and I may not ever understand it on this side of heaven. But it is through my limp that I can truly say, "It is through my weakness that God is strong."[74]

What I began to realize was my brokenness did not equate to worthlessness. I was not lower quality because of the cracks and fractures, those were simply where God's grace, mercy and power were able to shine. This is similar to how the Japanese value the kintsukuroi. *Kintsukuroi* is the Japanese art of repairing broken pottery with lacquer dusted or mixed with powdered gold, silver or platinum. As a philosophy, it treats

149

breakage as part of the history of an object, something to cherish rather than something to disguise.

"Kintsukuroi is similar to the Japanese philosophy of *wabi-sabi*, an embracing of the flawed or imperfect. They actually value the marks from wear by the use of an object. This can be seen as a rationale for keeping an object around even after it has been broken, highlighting the cracks and repairs as simply an event in the life of an object rather than allowing its service to end at the time of its damage or breakage. Not only is there no attempt to hide the damage, but the repair is literally illuminated."[75]

God began using my cracks and brokenness to help those who had also experienced suffering and loss. As I shared my pain with people, it gave them sparks of hope. I could see God's mercy and love cleaning and treating their wounds like a healing balm that flowed out of my brokenness. I see people who had hardened and walled-up hearts open like flowers the more vulnerable I am in sharing my story. The door of hope and freedom opened wide as I have allowed others to see and touch my wounds.

Everyone wants to appear flawless or like they have it altogether. This behavior seems even more prevalent in Christian circles which is opposite of God's design for us. Instead of trying to appear perfect, I believe God wants us to be transparent whether it's in our appearance, in our heart, our pain, or the deep wounds we have experienced.

Transparency brings healing. Just like the *kintsukuroi* pottery, God illuminates where we were damaged so He can shine His love and glory through those places and heal others. When we try to hide those broken parts of us, we also hide what He has done for us. In God's hands, our brokenness can be made into something beautiful. This is the great exchange. God transforms my broken pieces into something beautiful.

There's Gold in them Thar' Hills

"In God's Hands Intended Evil Becomes Eventual Good."[76]-Max Lucado

I heard someone recently say, "There's gold in them thar' hills." I really didn't know what that meant or where it came from. After doing a little research, I found out that it came from Mark Twain's books written while he was in California shortly after the Gold Rush. Mark Twain made it a catchphrase of the character Colonel Mulberry Sellers in his 1892 novel, *The American Claimant*.

To me, this saying reflects how God intentionally draws attention to the hidden treasures within our hearts that are waiting to be discovered. Those who are willing to allow others to see in have the opportunity to be healing vessels for the Lord in ways they never expected. God wants to use your rich seams of gold to bear witness of what happens when we surrender our pieces to Him.

When I allowed God to dig deep into my soul, He revealed the hidden treasures He had placed within me. He is the hidden treasure. When I didn't want anyone to see the real me, I was burying Jesus along with the junk. I was concealing Him. I was trying to disguise or hide my true self. I was hiding the true beauty within.

Can you imagine a new and beautiful five bedroom house you just bought? All the rooms are clean and spotless. It looks fantastic. But over a period of time, it accumulates trash. Instead of putting the trash out for pick-up, you start storing the trash in your basement and garage. Once those fill up, you start stuffing all your trash in the rooms.

Soon your rooms are filled with garbage and the house stinks like a garbage dump. Your house that was once new becomes unpleasant to live in. Suddenly, there's no more room for your garbage, you can't stand to live in your own house, but you don't know where to go. How do you fix it? You fix it by exchanging the trash that you were holding onto as if it were treasure for the real treasure, Jesus.

Healing the Heart

"Joseph (Genesis 50:20) *tied himself to the pillar of this promise and held on for dear life. Nothing in his story glosses over the presence of evil. Quite the contrary. Bloodstains, tearstains are everywhere. Joseph's heart was rubbed raw against the rocks of disloyalty and miscarried justice. Yet time and time again God redeemed the pain. The torn robe became a royal one. The pit became a palace. The broken family grew old together. The very acts intended to destroy God's servant turned out to strengthen him."*[77] *-Max Lucado*

In Genesis, we see that Joseph experienced great loss and God's redeeming path to heal and strengthen him enough to love even those who caused him the most injustice. His story resonated with me because of the tremendous amount of loss I had experienced throughout my life. Although my careless lifestyle brought on most of it, it was still authentic loss. A loss is a loss, no matter the cause, and a shattered heart is still a shattered heart even if we were the ones breaking it.

Shortly after my break up with Lori in 2003, someone at work dropped a bag of glitter pieces all over the floor. I remember looking down and thinking, "How am I ever going to find all these pieces of glitter and gather them and put them all back in the bag?" I was looking at all those pieces and it hit me that this was exactly the way I felt about my heart. It was all shattered into a million pieces. I wondered, "How in the world is my heart going to be put back together again?" and, "Could it even be repaired enough to live again, much less love again?" Thankfully, God found every piece of my heart and continues to put it back together again.

He knows what broke your heart. He is willing and able to gather up all the pieces of your broken life, mind, spirit, and heart. Jesus will love you back together again. His love holds all things together. Colossians 1:17 says, *"He is before all things, and in him all things hold together."*[78]

Not only that, but Jesus made my heart tender and soft again. "And I will give you a new heart, and I will put a new spirit in you. I will take out your stony, stubborn heart and give you a tender, responsive heart."[79] Jesus exchanged my hard and stony heart for a soft and pure heart. I can love again! And not just love, but I feel what He feels about others in His agape love, not just in my own limited human love.

It is Finished!

God, the Master Weaver. He stretches the yarn and intertwines the colors, the ragged twine with the velvet strings, the pains with the pleasures. Nothing escapes His reach. Every king, despot, weather pattern, and molecule are at His command. He passes the shuttle back and forth across the generations, and as He does, a design emerges. Satan weaves; God reweaves.

The idea of God reweaving what Satan weaved is not a 20th century statement. Joseph made a similar statement when he said. "You intended to harm me, but God intended it for good to accomplish what is now being done, the saving of many lives."- Genesis 50:20 (NIV) *When Joseph said, "you intended harm" or also translated "you meant evil against me" he was using a Hebrew word that traces its meaning to 'weave' or 'plait.' In essence he was saying, "you wove evil, but God rewove it together for good."[80]* -Max Lucado

God gave me a similar revelation a few years ago. I was a full-time missionary with Family Missions Company out of Abbeville, Louisiana in 2011. We endured some intense spiritual training while in the intake process. The intake was three months of training and growing in community. It was like a spiritual boot camp. God did amazing things within my heart, and the hearts of my brothers and sisters from my intake community. It was a beautiful time of healing my heart with the body of Christ. I also experienced joy unspeakable while living as a missionary. God exchanged my old empty life for a fulfilled life of joy and adventure!

One weekend, during my intake process, we had a "Life in the Spirit" day retreat. We prayed for a release of the Holy Spirit in a new way. We prayed for a fresh outpouring of the Holy Spirit while we were separated into groups and praying over each other. As they laid hands on me, there were many beautiful prophecies spoken over me. One woman spoke over me saying, "Jesus says, "It is finished, Dana. It is done!"

A few hours later, after our retreat concluded, we all gathered together to celebrate by having a picnic at the park. It was a beautiful sunny day and we were all finding our places on the grass. We had blankets that we laid out to sit on.

A fifteen-year-old boy, who happened to be the son of the woman who prophesied over me, ran up to me as we were preparing to eat. I will never forget the look in his eyes.

"Dana, while we were praying for someone in my group, I looked across the room and could only see you. Jesus showed me a vision for you, Dana," he said with excitement and slight hesitation. "Do you want me to share it with you now?"

Of course I did. I even forgot about my my food, which is a miracle because I love to eat. I knew he had something very important to share with me. I said, "Yes, now is good!"

This was his vision as I remember it:

He saw Jesus dressed in white, and right beside him was the devil dressed in black. There was a table set before them with a large puzzle on it which consisted of black and white pieces. The puzzle had gaps and missing pieces because the puzzle wasn't finished. Jesus had the white pieces and the devil had the black pieces. Every time Jesus put a white piece in the puzzle the devil would put a black piece in.

One by one, they continued. Jesus would put in a white piece and then the devil would put in a black piece. As they were putting the pieces in the puzzle, they started going faster and faster and faster. It was almost like a race. Jesus finally had had enough, and he violently overturned the table causing the puzzle and the devil to be destroyed. As he was flipping the table, Jesus said, "IT IS FINISHED! It is finished!"

As he shared this vision with me, the tears just fell. It was exactly what I had been going through. There was so much revealed to me through this vision. First, if Jesus says, "It is finished," then it is finished. Second, the white pieces signified the truth Jesus was speaking over me and the black pieces were all the lies and accusations the enemy kept throwing at me. I was in a battle in my mind.

The puzzle represented my life: past, present and future. The puzzle wasn't completed because neither is my life. Jesus was furious at the lies the enemy had been throwing at me for such a long time causing me much confusion, torment and pain. Jesus, in all His love and power, turned the table on my enemy. He was contending and fighting for me. It was such a vivid picture of God's wrath and holy vengeance against my enemy, the devil.

The boy with the vision said, "Jesus was mad, Dana."

This reminded me of when Jesus, in Matthew 21:12, overthrew the tables of the moneychangers. He was angry. He had a holy, righteous anger against the evildoers in His house. Jesus was assuring me that it was finished when he shed his blood for me and I needed that revelation.

I needed to see Jesus was fighting for me and to be reminded it is a finished work. Although Jesus' blood paid the price, I have to constantly stand and walk in that truth. I have to be intentional in my thinking, every day. I have to stand on God's word every day, every hour. I am aware the enemy is prowling around like a lion looking for someone to devour. He may try to whisper lies and try to trip me up, but I will continue to stand on the word of God and stand in His truth. I choose to counterattack using the word of God. I see now the thing the enemy says is the complete opposite of what God says. The truth sets me free so that I can live in His freedom. It is finished.

Jesus has been so faithful to me by filling in all the missing pieces of my past. He used Desert Stream Ministries, a healing place for the sexually and relationally wounded, as a place where I could be raw and real and find answers to so many questions from my childhood, my lesbian past, and addictions. I wanted to see things for what they were in the light of God's truth and love. I needed answers, but not just answers, I needed God's truth to fill in all those gaps from my past. God continues to fill them in with His truth and love.

It has been a sweet but painful process, and I am determined to see the truth in every area of my life. Like the woman determined to touch Jesus' hem, I am determined to receive my healing and become a new creation in every area of my life. I am continually amazed at how God is restoring and uncovering me, and bringing to light all that was suppressed or hidden. I invite you to enter into the great exchange with God. Exchange your lies, self-protection, rejection, and overall brokenness for His truth, protection, acceptance, and most importantly, His love

—9—
Real Talk

Dearly Beloved

This chapter is personally written to the ones who identify as a lesbian, homosexual, transgender, struggling with same sex attraction, and/or other identity related issues.

My Dearly Beloved Friends,

I have good news for you! I love you and my heart is for you. First and foremost, I want to stand in as an ambassador for the body of Christ. I stand as a humble representative and ask for forgiveness for the many ways we have failed to love you. Forgive those of us who have not reflected the love of Christ to you as a person and those of us who have judged, criticized, or condemned you.

I ask forgiveness for the times you felt misunderstood or rejected by the Church rather than loved and accepted for who you are. I ask forgiveness for the hurt and pain your parents may have caused you for not being able to understand you, for judging you and/or for disowning you. These actions are not a reflection of Jesus' love, and I sincerely ask you to forgive me, and the body of Christ, for hurting you.

My beloved, I love you, but God loves you more. He loves you more than you love yourself. You are made by His design, in His image and likeness. You are a reflection of the glory of God. His love is revealed through your unique, one-of-a-kind personhood as male or female. No one will ever replace or replicate you. You are one in a million. No one created before you or after you can be duplicated, and no one can contribute to the world exactly what God has placed in you, except you. God loves you as He created you.

I simply desire to share my heart with you, personally. I hope to be a voice that makes a way for you to know how Jesus feels about you in a way that you have never known before. This is the very essence of why I am writing to you directly.

While living in the lesbian lifestyle, I would have given anything for someone who had been there to come alongside and show me a way out. I longed for a voice who would call me out and into my true identity in Christ. I desperately longed to hear the voice of truth and love that challenged me to an authentic and abundant life in Christ.

I care about you. I want you to know that God's truth and love are braided together and cannot be separated. I want to echo some of these truths that God revealed to me, but by the same token, without beating you up with them. My hope is that you would see my heart opening up to you, and know my heart is for you. Here are some of the questions I had while living in the lesbian lifestyle along with my current understanding of answers based on scripture and revelation.

The Gift

Who am I, really?

"The idea of knowing ourselves opens us up to an ocean of questions about the purpose of our existence. Such questions have captivated man since ancient times."[81]
- Jason & Crystalina Evert and Brian Butler

I had a vision while living in the convent in 1997. At the time, I was kneeling before Jesus in the Adoration Chapel in San Antonio, Texas. As I was looking up at Him, I had a vision of a big, wrapped Christmas present. I started to tear into this beautiful gift, and as I unwrapped it, I discovered that the gift inside was Jesus. There was layer upon layer of wrapping paper as if it was an endless gift before me. It seemed like I would never get through all this gift. As I peeled back each layer of wrapping paper, I would discover another beautiful treasure hidden inside.

The love of Jesus flowing through this endless gift opening experience was overwhelming. I realized that this gift was not only Jesus, but it was His sacred heart. While I was opening each layer of this beautiful gift, I began to see through Jesus' eyes what a gift I am to Him and to the body of Christ. The more I opened this gift, the more I understood His love for me. Jesus' heart has so many layers that it would take an eternity to know the height and depth of His great love for me. Jesus is the gift, the priceless treasure. He gave Himself as a gift to me when he was sacrificed on the cross.

You, my friend, are a gift waiting to be unwrapped by the Father. Deep inside of you are hidden treasures and gifts from God. There are treasures hidden there you probably haven't discovered or tapped into yet. These treasures can only be opened and discovered in the sacred place where you and God meet. The Holy Spirit wants to unveil the beauty and value you hold inside of you.

Adam, in the book of Genesis, would connect and talk with God in the Garden of Eden. That was their sacred place of communing together. There is a sacred place in your heart that is set aside for God alone. No other person can meet you there. He desperately wants to love on you and reveal Himself to you. He will help you to see what He sees and feel what He feels about you. You will discover who you are, whose you are, and what you are made for in that secret place with Him. He knows you like no other because He is the one who created you.

While living my life completely surrendered to God, I have discovered treasures deep within that I longed to see my whole life. "This relationship with God is defined by that unique fact that the more deeply I abandon myself to Him, the more deeply I let Him penetrate my being, the more powerfully He, the Creator, gains authority in me, the more I become myself."[82] He has unveiled my heart and has allowed me to feel what he feels and see what he sees through His eyes, about me. In this intimacy with Jesus, I see my reflection. I see the "true Dana" that I'm created to be when filtered by His love.

Who Do You Say I am?

In Matthew 16:13, it says, *"Jesus came into the region of Caesarea Philippi. He asked His disciples, saying, 'Who do men say that I am?'"*[83] There was a lot of gossip and talk about Jesus, but He wanted His disciples to KNOW clearly who He was. The disciples first answered Jesus, "Some say, John the Baptist; others say Elijah; and still others say you are one of the prophets." Jesus was probably thinking, that is everyone's opinion, "But who do you say I am?" Peter finally answered, "You are the Christ." That is truly who Jesus was and is. He is the Messiah, the Savior of the world!

I invite you into one of my prayers for revelation:

"Father God, you know me. You are my creator. You know my heart. You know my pain. You know my deepest longings even before I am aware of them. Jesus, I don't know who I am, but you do. Jesus, I don't have the answers to life's deepest questions, but you do. You know me and you have sought me out, because of your great love for me. Jesus, I am desperate for you! I want to know you. I am so tired of trying to figure things out on my own. I need your help,

Oh God, I need you. I need you Holy Spirit. Please, come into my heart and reveal yourself to me. Jesus, I come boldly to you. Jesus, who do you say that I am? Who am I, Jesus? Please show me. Jesus, I want to see what you see in me, and feel what you feel about me." Amen.

One of Saint Pope John Paul II's favorite phrases in the Second Vatican Council was, "It is Jesus, the Son of God, who fully reveals man to himself and brings to light his most high calling."

84

What is humanity's highest calling? It is to be and know who you are as a son or daughter of the Most High God. It is not enough to just acknowledge that God is your father. I learned that it was only through humility, in surrendering my will over to God that He could then reveal my true or authentic identity to me. After surrendering and letting go of me and my will, and after I received the baptism of the Holy Spirit, I then knew my identity as a child of the Most High God. After receiving His Holy Spirit, I could cry out, "Abba Father" and receive the fullness of His adoption.

God revealed to me that I had a stony and hardened heart. Before I turned back to God, I couldn't make my heart soft, pliable, or teachable. God handed me over to the lust of my desires and passions after the many times I rejected His guidance. Through my healing journey, the Lord spoke to me and revealed that my heart was like that of Pharaoh's heart, hard and obstinate toward God. I didn't think of myself as being hard-hearted and stubborn, but now I see that I was.

After God filled me with His Spirit, the scales fell off my eyes and I could see again. Sin was numbing my heart causing it to callous. It was the power of God's love that broke those thick callouses off. You or I cannot accomplish this by your own good deeds or intentions. The power of God's love is the only thing that can melt our hearts of stone and can give us a soft and pliable heart.

In Romans 8:15-16, Paul explains that the Holy Spirit reveals to us our deepest identity as son or daughter of God, giving us confidence to cry out, "Abba, Father!" It is the revelation of God's unconditional love that enables a person to fully accept who they are as a man or woman created in God's image. But by embracing our identity, we can become free to fulfill our destiny"[85]

I want to encourage you to know your true identity in Christ, to become free to fulfill your calling or destiny. I want to warn you that there is a real thief, the enemy of our soul, whose only purpose on this earth is to steal, kill, and destroy all of God's holy and pure intentions for you.[86] The devil is the father of lies, and in him there is no truth, only deceit. He wants to steal you, the good and holy gift God created you to be.

The enemy of your soul wants you to believe that you were a mistake by being born as the wrong gender. He doesn't want you to discover who you really are in Christ. He wants you to reject yourself, the beautiful you that God made. He knit you with His loving hands when He formed you in the womb and He makes no mistakes.

The enemy doesn't want you to be unveiled by God's love and truth. He wants you to be imprisoned by his deceit and lies that are opposed to God's love and truth. The devil's ultimate goal is for you to stay opposed to God. As long as the enemy can trap you into this heart attitude of rejection to your very self, you will stay in a state of rejecting God. If you reject yourself, you will reject the One who made you. The enemy doesn't want you free in your identity as a son or daughter of God which is why it is critical that we find that place with God where we can be confident and sure of our identity.

When I am in my secret place with Jesus, I don't have to hide anymore. I can be completely exposed in the light of His presence and love. I am uncovered by his love for me. It is in that vulnerability of being bare before Jesus, that I am free. It is in this naked surrender I am transparent before God. As I decrease (my self-will, desires, wants, etc.), His love increases. I become more and more of who I am created to be as I allow myself to be in relationship with Jesus. In that sacred place, I am free to be me in every way.

In the light of His truth and love, I am free with no limits. I am free to be a whole and holy gift with no hindrances of striving for attention or acceptance. I am fully embraced, accepted, and loved. It is in relationship with Jesus that I'm affirmed, accepted and loved for being beautiful me.

Born This Way? By Design?

Maybe you have heard or said something like this regarding the homosexual lifestyle:

*"God is My Heavenly Father. He loves me.
This is the way 'He made me.' He wants
me to be happy, right? I know it must be
right because this lifestyle makes me
happy."*

When God created us, He found mankind to be "very good."[87] God knew that it was not good for Adam to be alone, so He created Eve as a suitable partner for him. They were made in God's image and likeness. God created man and woman for one another as a perfect and suitable gift to each other. Adam complimented Eve in His masculinity and Eve complimented Adam with her femininity.

In the beginning, the original nakedness of Adam and Eve was a peaceful state because there was no struggle to love.[88] It was natural for Adam and Eve to be naked and to love rather than to lust after each other. At this point, everything was still pure, including the heart of man. St. Pope John Paul II said, "Their nakedness, combined with original innocence, allowed Adam and Eve to be naked without shame."[89]

Adam and Eve's naked bodies revealed their call to make a gift of themselves to each other, because God had made them with a purity of heart. St. Pope John Paul II calls this kind of purity, the "nuptial meaning of the body."[90] In the physical design of their bodies, Adam and Eve saw that their bodies literally fit together; they knew that they were made for a physical communion that was holy and sanctified. Adam and Eve were free to reflect the attributes of God by giving themselves to one another. St. Pope John Paul II describes "original unity" as the "initial experience of perfect unity between man and woman."[91]

Adam and Eve shared a complete integration of the soul and body and experienced a deep unity of will and holy sexual desire. Their bodies responded in perfect unity with their wills, allowing them to love each other rightly. Their sexual desire sprang from an authentic love. (Later, I will describe how original sin caused us to fall into a state of conflict, confusion, and dis-integration.)

The second chapter of Genesis closes with an important teaching of how marriage came to exist. Genesis 2:24 says, *"Therefore a man leaves his father and his mother and cleaves to his wife, and they become one flesh."[92]* It goes on to tell us that "The man and his wife were both naked, and were not ashamed." They were not ashamed because they were in this union of holy marriage instituted by God. This is God's original and authentic plan for humankind, man and woman designed for one another in a sacred union of holy marriage.

When God gave Eve as a gift to Adam, I would guess that Adam exclaimed, "This is now bone of my bone and flesh of my flesh." "The happiness of Adam and Eve came through living and loving in marriage as God loves: freely, totally, faithfully, and fruitfully. We are all made to live and experience this same "original happiness" God designed for us."[93]

Here's another scenario:

> *If God's beautiful design for sex and marriage is as Genesis describes it, then why are people so confused about marriage, sexual orientation, and experience desires that are contrary to what God designed?*

I personally wrestled with this question for years while living in the lesbian lifestyle. If God created me to be with a man in marriage, why did I struggle with same-sex attraction? After being out of the lesbian lifestyle for over a decade now, I have received revelation through personal prayer and the word of God that has helped me understand.

First, I discovered that the sin of our first parents, Adam and Eve, brought strong sexual desire into the world. It started with the simple choice of going with their own plan instead of God's plan. Their original sin has affected us all. "Instead of wanting to do what's right, we often desire to do wrong."[94] This tendency to sin is called concupiscence.

"Concupiscence basically means lust, a disorder in our desires, a tendency for our desires to be misdirected toward what is opposed to God's will, toward what may seem to make us happy, but actually hinders our true happiness."[95] God designed for us to have "original and authentic happiness" by living and loving in holy marriage as God instituted. However, even that comes after living in full communion with God.

In reference to concupiscence or misdirected/twisted desires, there are many forms in which these disordered desires can manifest. Same-sex attraction is only one of the many forms such disorder can take.[96] There are disordered desires for approval, greed, material possessions, self-absorption, vanity, food, drinking and heterosexual sex, etc.[97]

The question rises for those with same-sex attraction,

are you born this way?

Because of original sin, we are all born with an inclination to various misdirected or twisted desires. We are all shaped and formed uniquely by our inherited makeup, character, upbringing, personal family history, and especially the culture in which we live. Mary Healy says,

> "None of us is born with a God-given orientation to the same sex. God does not give people an orientation that is at odds with the design of their body and that makes it impossible for them to achieve sexual union or bring forth new life. We are all born wounded by original sin, which is then compounded by our own sin and the sins and failures of others inflicted on us. But our wounds do not define who we are."[98]

No, God didn't make me to desire and be sexually attracted to women. I was not born gay. God, our loving Father would not give me an orientation contrary to His original design that would produce life.

177

In essence, homosexuality is a learned behavior. Our loving Father would not and does not create a person to be gay. It is simple. God intentionally crafts you perfectly within His holy design as a reflection of Himself. It is not in His character to create someone who cannot function within that design. Think about it in this perspective. If I say that I was born gay, it would be the same as saying I was born as an alcoholic, a murderer, a prostitute, or a habitual liar. We are not born drinking alcohol out of our mother's womb. We are not born wanting to kill someone. We are not born desiring to sell our body for money. We are not born telling lies to get what we want. All of these familiar habits and/or addictions are learned behaviors that help us cope or deal with pain, loss, worthlessness, rejection, anger, abandonment and so on.

Let's be real. All of these alternate ways of living are not God's design for us. It pains me to see people living out of their wounded and broken mindsets. Each one of us deals with our pain in different ways. Our brokenness manifests in different ways, through many different outlets and the enemy of our soul wants it to be a bondage of some shape or form. If the devil can't get you in one area, he will try an alternate route.

Like any other misdirected desire, the path of least resistance is through our weaknesses and wounds. It is there that we are most susceptible or prone to inordinate desires and feelings. Same-sex attraction is just one of the ways the enemy twists what is holy and pure, especially in our sexual identity. God created us to have sexual desires. Sexual drive is natural and even holy. God made us to enjoy sexual pleasure in the context of holy marriage between a man and a woman.

When I was living in a sexual relationship with another woman, there were many feelings I experienced that supported my beliefs that my lifestyle was morally right. Although those feelings were powerful, they were also fleeting. Physical pleasure only lasts for a moment. They only feed our fleshly desires, and the pleasures of those sins are brief.

We can't honestly determine if homosexual practice is morally right simply if it feels right. The same is true for a married person. If he or she becomes sexually involved with someone besides his or her spouse, it may feel good for the moment, but that doesn't make it right.

Looking back, I see that the momentary pleasures that came from my lesbian relationships always left me feeling like I had no life within me. I felt dry, empty and dead in my spirit. Sex outside of God's fantastic and holy plan is lifeless and leaves you feeling empty. It is selfish, not sacrificial. It is lust, not love. In hindsight, these relationships were always self-gratifying and in no way life-giving. I was always left wanting more. Like any addiction, it never satisfied me, no matter what.

> *"It is Jesus that you seek when you dream of happiness; He is waiting for you when nothing else satisfies you; He is the beauty to which you are so attracted; it is he who provoked you with that thirst for fullness that will not let you settle for compromise; it is he who urges you to shed the mask of a false life; it is he who reads in your hearts your most genuine choices, the choices that others try to stifle. It is Jesus who stirs in you the desire to do something great with your lives, the will to follow an ideal, the refusal to allow yourselves to be ground by mediocrity, the courage to commit yourselves and society, making the world more human and fraternal." – St. Pope John Paul II[99]*

Scenario:

> *"What's so bad about being in a relationship with another woman? I'm not hurting anyone. As long as I love her, I'm not doing anything wrong. I'm committed to her and our relationship."*

In my past lesbian relationships, I became obsessed with the creation, rather than the God the creator. In Romans 1:25 it says, *"They exchanged the truth of God for a lie, and worshipped and served created things rather than the Creator."*[100] My sexual partners became my gods and idols. I placed my relationships with them over everything, including my relationship with God. I placed them ahead of the very first commandment, "Thou shalt have no other gods before me."[101]

I have learned that in order to love well and pure heartedly, I have to get rid of any and all idols. Idolatry ultimately results in the worship of self, placing what we want over what God wants. On the other hand, when we obey and honor God first, everything else falls into place and order because that is the way that God created us to operate. We can be at peace with ourselves when we are functioning in His ordered design.

I rejoice in healthy and holy friendships, especially with other women. God has changed my heart and the way I see other women. I am able to love them as friends, the way God originally intended for me to. I no longer see people (women or men) as something to appease my own selfish desires. I never intentionally set out to be selfish in my friendships or relationships. Whereas before, I did whatever I could to get my emotional, sexual, quick fixes in order to fill those voids and gaps in my heart.

It is by living in relationship with God that each of us is a good gift to the body of Christ. I have such great joy living in the freedom from emotional, sexual, and alcohol addiction. I am so happy to be a safe place for women now. I also have a joy and freedom from having healthy and holy boundaries with friends. I desire to see people who are struggling have this same freedom.

"I'm Not That Special"

Is there a way out of same sex attraction and addiction?

When I first dabbled in the lesbian lifestyle at nineteen, I remember feeling wrong because I wanted to hide everything I was doing. I internally questioned, "If this is good or right, then why do I want to hide everything I'm doing?" When I would go out to a gay bar, it was always so secretive. No one could know about my secret. My friends and I lived by hiding in the dark. I sensed what I was doing wasn't right. It didn't feel right.

I used to lie about everything. My whole life felt like a big lie. I was hiding from my parents, friends, and family because deep in my subconscious I knew it wasn't right to be with another woman. It wasn't right, and that's why I wanted to hide it. It wasn't right to get drunk either, and that's why I was hiding the alcohol, too.

After living in that lifestyle for such a long time, it numbed my conscience. I justified my sinful actions, soothed my own conscience, and silenced my inner plea to fully submit to God and His word. I tried to rationalize the truth in every area of my life especially relating to my identity as a lesbian and my sexuality. I exhausted my efforts in trying to beat my conscience into submission trying to avoid the torment of conviction.

Adam and Eve hid after they disobeyed God. It was through disobeying God and discovering their own sin that they realized that they were naked. Adam and Eve's first response was to cover themselves up. They felt the shame of sin immediately after they disobeyed God and experienced the first consequence of their sin which was the loss of sexual innocence.

The same desire to hide, shame and loss of innocence is true for the sexual sinner and addict. Sexual sin has such a deep sense of shame attached to its behaviors which is why 1 Corinthians 6:18 says, *"Run from sexual sin! No other sin so clearly affects the body as this one does. For sexual immorality is a sin against your own body."*[102]

Sin harms our spirit by dividing our hearts. It fractures our relationship with God. It's the same with any sin, but especially sexual sin. I was ashamed of my sexual perversion and secret addictions. However, I found hope when I brought my sin into the light.

Years ago, I was sharing my conversion story with a friend who was in the lesbian lifestyle. I told her I was currently living a life of chastity and purity unto God by His grace.

"Well, Dana, you are holy, or special. You can live a pure and chaste life because you are extraordinary. I can't do that. I can't live without having sex."

She implied that she felt it was more possible for me because I had a special dose of grace or holiness when really she was trying to excuse her own behavior and explain why she couldn't surrender to God.

I'm not that special. I am simply a person who is totally surrendered to Jesus Christ. There is no favoritism with God. Romans 2:11 says, *"For there is no partiality with God."*[103] The good news is that we are all His favorites. God has made all of us in His image and likeness. He chose all of us to follow Him. You are made to live out this kind of life. You were made to give your all to Him and be His bride.

In 1 Peter 2:9 it says, *"But you are a chosen people, a royal priesthood, a holy nation, God's special possession, that you may declare the praises to him who called you out of darkness into his wonderful light."*[104] As His children, we are all called to this holy family. We are all called to love Him who has first loved us. *"Be holy as He is holy."*[105] There are no special exemptions. You are called to the same holiness, purity, and chastity that I am called to.

The Invitation

As you have read, these were some common questions and thoughts that I tried to justify and rationalize with to silence my inner turmoil. Thankfully, they could not overcome the invitation extended by Jesus Christ.

Matthew 22:14 says, *"Many are called but few are chosen."*[106] This statement was the conclusion to the parable of the wedding feast. Jesus used this parable to show what the Kingdom of Heaven was like. In the parable, the king sends his servants out to gather the wedding guests to the feast. But those invited refused to come, some because they were too busy with their own worldly pursuits and endeavors.

Some of those that refuse chose the lust of their own hearts over God. Romans 1:26-27 says,

> *"Therefore, God handed them over to degrading passions. Their females exchanged natural relations with unnatural, and the males likewise gave up natural relations with females and burned for lust of one another. Males did shameful things with males and thus received in their own persons the due penalty for their perversity."*[107]

'In order to expose the depth of humanity's rebellion against the Creator, God handed them over to impurity

186

through the lusts of their hearts. Instead of curbing people's evil interest, God abandoned them to self-indulgence, thereby removing the façade of deceptive conformity to divine will." [108] God will allow you to choose. He does not choose for you.

Some refuse because they were unreceptive toward the king. In Ephesians 4:18, it says, *"They are darkened in their understanding, alienated from the life of God because of the ignorance that is in them, due to their hardness of heart."[109]* Friend, my desire is that you would not fall into either of these categories. I pray that you would be one to receive and accept God's invitation.

Revelations 3:20 *"Behold, I stand at the door and knock. If anyone hears my voice and opens the door, I will come in to him and eat with him, and he with me."[110]*

Jesus is inviting you to follow Him. He is knocking at the door of your heart. You may even feel uncomfortable as you are reading this now because this is confirmation of something you have felt for a while now. God is persistent and faithful to chase you down until you are His, wholly and completely. He is jealous for you and your love.

If you have never been invited to follow Jesus, I'm personally inviting you now. The invitation is in your hands, with your name written on it. You are chosen to live a life that is holy and pure, and do great things for the kingdom of God.

A Prayer for Salvation:

Father God, I come to you just as I am. There is something drawing me to answer your call on my life. I may not understand fully at this time, but I accept the invitation you have presented to me. I want to come to you. I want you to unveil the real me through your love. I also desire for you to show me who You are. I want to know you, Jesus. I want to follow you, but I have some fears or hesitations.

I believe in you, Jesus, but please help my unbelief. Help me to trust that you know what is best for me. I can't put it off for one more day. I can't resist your love. I have been running from you my whole life and I am so tired of running. I give up, Lord! I let go, Jesus. I have so many questions but I choose to believe in faith that you will answer them in your timing.

Jesus, I confess that I am a sinner in need of a Savior. Save me! Help me! Jesus, I believe that you died on the cross and shed your blood for me. I confess that you are My Lord and Savior. I ask you to forgive me for all my sins, known and unknown. Wash me, cleanse me, and save me, Jesus.

I desire to know you and want to seek you daily. I want you to deliver me from all my sins and addictions. I give my life to you. I give my heart to you, Jesus. I ask you to wash me with your love. Take my stony heart and make it like your heart, Jesus. I want to feel what you feel and see what you see, when you look at me.

Jesus, touch me and heal me. Make me whiter than snow. You know my heart. You know my thoughts. You know my pain, Jesus. You know me! Give me a clean heart and renew a steadfast spirit within me. I choose you today, Jesus. Please, give me the grace I need to trust you. Jesus, I trust in your love for me. Amen.

—10—

Contending for Your Loved One

"When someone you love embraces homosexuality, you immediately begin doing battle with despair. The enemy goes after you. The only force great enough to defeat his efforts is God alone."[111] *- Lou Franklin*

Be Gentle

Are you a parent with a child that has embraced homosexuality? As a parent, your initial response might be guilt or a sense of responsibility. What did I do? Where did I go wrong? First and foremost, be merciful to yourself. God sees your every effort in parenting the best you know how. He sees how much you sacrificed and provided for your children in ways that they may never know or see on this side of Heaven. God is merciful. He loves you. He knows that you are not perfect and knew that you would fall short as a parent. He knows every single weakness you struggle with.

I give you permission to receive God's mercy, to allow Him to pour His love upon your pain, anger, fear and guilt. In Jesus' name, I release God's love and mercy in your heart now. As you receive, it will allow you to give love and mercy to your child which they need now, more than ever.

Be Brave

In John 16:33, Jesus says, *"I have told you this so that you might have peace in me. In the world you will have trouble, but take courage, I have conquered the world."[112]*

Be brave. Come to the Lord with a humble heart and open yourself up to His truth and love. You have permission to ask the difficult questions about why this situation has manifested. Ask God, "Why? Why is my daughter living a lesbian lifestyle, my son living a homosexual lifestyle? Why does my daughter want to be a man and have a sex change? You are the Creator, God. You didn't make a mistake when you made my son as a male, and my daughter as female. So why is this happening, Lord? I need answers, God. I need your help. Show me your truth in all of this confusion."

Take courage. God desires to give you understanding. He wants to answer your questions and give you clarity in the chaos and confusion of homosexuality. Confusion is not from God. Confusion is a way the enemy keeps your head spinning round and round with no clear vision causing a whirlwind of chaos. The chaos leaves you feeling like you will never find your footing causing despair and hopelessness. My prayer for you is that in Jesus' name, all confusion will break off you and you will receive God's peace and clarity in your mind.

1 Corinthians 14:33 says, *"For God is not a God of confusion, but of peace."*[113]

2 Timothy 2:7 says, *"Think over what I say, for the Lord will give you understanding in everything."*[114]

Through the Eyes of God

"We cannot agree that the 'gay self' is an inspired destiny for him or her. Rather, we cry out to God and ask for **authentic sight***, that we might see this one in the light of God's fruitful intentions for him or her."*[115] *- Andrew Comiskey*

It is vital for you as a parent to see your child as God sees them, as His beautiful creation, His holy, intended design. God sees His people as he created them, a finished product, complete and whole. God looks at us and sees no flaws, wounds, or baggage. He sees us through the blood of Jesus, clothed in His righteousness.

You must first see your child through the eyes of Jesus so that you can understand how He sees you. In seeing through the eyes of Jesus, it will help you align your thoughts, emotions and words with His truth about who they are. In doing this, you will be able to extend that same mercy and tenderness to your child.

I encourage you to be patient with the process of healing and wholeness for both you and your child. Remember, God's timing is not the same as your timing. Although you may know some things about your child, you don't know their every thought or feeling.[116] Only God knows all the details of their heart, and only He can meet them in that secret place and bring complete healing and restoration.

Walk by faith, believing that God is working diligently behind the scenes in your child. Let God be God. He doesn't need your help in disciplining them. Sometimes God is waiting for you to get out of His way so He can reveal Himself to your child. Your job is to trust that God is the best parent, and He knows exactly how to navigate your child's heart and mind with love.

Love and accept them just as they are, with no strings attached. Love unconditionally. Trust in Jesus. Trust in His perfect leadership. The Holy Spirit will lead you and guide you in how to communicate with your child. He only needs your cooperation in letting Him be God in your life, and in your child's life as well.

God is relentless in His pursuit of us. He is faithful to you and your child. His ultimate commitment to us was demonstrated on the cross at Calvary. The blood he shed was His proof of undying love and commitment to us. He is enough! In your lament over your child's present lifestyle choice, or for any of the pain or grief you are experiencing, I encourage you to grab hold of the cross of Jesus. Allow yourself to become undone at His feet. Allow yourself to grieve over the loss. You had dreams for your child, and it is understandable to feel disappointed and a deep sense of loss. It can even feel like a death. However, when you grieve, hold onto hope that you will see your child once again live in complete freedom and wholeness.

In Mark's gospel, there was a Jewish leader named Jairus. One day, his 12-year-old daughter was ill to the point of nearly dying. He was completely hopeless. Mark 5:21-24 says,

> *"Jesus went across the sea of Galilee in a*
> *boat. It landed at the other side. There a*

large crowd gathered around Him. Then a man named Jairus came. He was a synagogue ruler. Seeing Jesus, he fell at His feet. He begged Jesus, 'Please come. My little daughter is dying. Place your hands on her to heal her. Then she will live.' So Jesus went with him."[117]

I want to point out a few things to you from this beautiful picture of Jairus falling at Jesus' feet in his hopeless situation. This was no small act for Jairus. He wasn't just inviting Jesus over for a cup of tea. His little girl's life was fading fast! Imagine the sight of Jairus falling at Jesus' feet and begging him to come and heal his little girl. Jairus had faith that Jesus could heal his daughter and make her whole again. Jesus loved Jairus and did not hesitate to go with him.

Jesus is full of compassion. He feels the pain His people feel. Jesus was pleased that Jairus had faith to come to Him in his hopelessness.[118] Jesus feels every bit of the pain you feel. Like Jairus, have the faith that Jesus can revive your child and they will be forever changed. Do not be afraid to fall at the feet of Jesus and contend for the healing and salvation of your child. He has the power to help you when no one else can. He knows exactly what you need when you cry for help and His hand is not too short to save.

Jesus' blood and sacrifice is enough to set people free from any bondage, addiction or sin. Jesus himself went down to the hell so that we could rise in new life with Him. There is no valley or far off place that is too deep or too dark for God. He can reach your child no matter how far away they may seem, or how long you have believed for their freedom and wholeness. Remember, God is long-suffering. Watch and wait for His promises to be fulfilled in your children's lives.

Doubting God's Goodness

In your pain, it can be easy to want to accuse God of all sorts of things. But remember, our enemy is the accuser. He wants us to doubt God's goodness, love and commitment to us. Revelation 12:10 says,

> *"Then I heard a loud voice from heaven say: Now have salvation and power come, and the kingdom of our God and the authority of his Anointed. For the accuser of our brothers is cast out, who accuses them before our God day and night."* [119]

The enemy hates God. He wants us to become embittered against Him and ultimately hate as well. The enemy may whisper a question like, "God, how could you sit around and let this happen to my child?" Or, "Where were you when these bad influences came into their life? I thought I could trust you, God." If the pain isn't dealt with, and you come in agreement with the enemy's lies, you can become embittered against God.

The truth is that God does care about every pain and wound in our hearts. He wants you to invite Him into that deep pain. Be real and honest with God. Be raw. God can take it. Remember, Jesus bore the weight of our sin on the cross, He can surely take on our deepest hurt and pain.

Check yourself now, and see if there are any bitter roots in your heart that oppose God's goodness, faithfulness, truth, and love for you. Be honest with yourself. If your beliefs and thoughts are not lining up with the word of God, then you are more than likely believing the lies of the enemy. Do all you can to keep your heart clear of the enemies lies.

Directing Your Anger

Anger is a natural emotion that comes when we are disappointed, hurt, wounded or when we just don't know

198

all the answers in life. It is an emotion that God gave us. It is ok to get mad or angry if it doesn't lead to sin.

Ephesians 4:26 says, *"In your anger do not sin. Do not let the sun go down while you are still angry."*[120]

Don't let anger have control over you or take root in your heart. Whenever we are wounded and feel anger stirring inside us, the scheme of the enemy is to have us direct our anger onto God. Hebrews 12:15 says, *"Looking diligently lest anyone fall short of the grace of God; lest any root of bitterness springing up cause trouble, and by this many become defiled."*[121]

We must be quick to recognize and detect the bitter roots that may spring up in our hearts. We must be diligent to remove bitterness from our hearts because its powerful influence can quickly trouble us with pain and may ruin many of our relationships.

Once we take our pain and disappointment's personally, we invite the forces of evil to win us over. I want you to see what is taking place.[122] This is a spiritual matter. In Ephesians 6:12, Paul says,

> *"For our struggle is not against flesh and blood, but against the rulers, against the*

authorities, against the power of this dark world and against the spiritual forces of evil in the heavenly realms."[123]

Remember, the devil is in the business of destroying families. He will come around in any way, shape, or form he can. He uses our hurts to try to damage us and our relationships. 1 Peter 5:8 says, *"Stay Alert! Watch out for your great enemy, the devil. He prowls around like a roaring lion, looking for someone to devour."* [124] As Christians, we have to be aware of the enemy's deception and schemes. We must be a people of discernment and prayer, always watching and alert.

Keep your eyes fixed on Jesus during these disruptive and malicious attacks from the enemy. See what is taking place spiritually. As a Christian, you are in a battle whether you like it or not. You have to continuously choose which side you stand on. The enemy would love to see you fall into his trap, direct your pain onto your daughter or son, and cause division and irreparable damage. He would love it if you rejected, disowned, or judged your child because it would mean that he won.

If this is something you have done in the past, I want to encourage you that all is not lost. Even if you have not said or done all the right things, God can heal and restore. His love holds all things together.

After all these years, I have finally directed my anger in the right direction against the one who stole from me. The devil is the one we should aim all our anger towards. As Christians, we fight with the fire of God burning in our hearts. That is how the battle is won, by loving one another in truth and in His love.

Restitution

Restitution is a biblical concept from both the Old and New Testaments that reveal the heart of God on this subject. In the Old Testament, the Israelites were under the law, which specified restitution in a variety of circumstances: *"If a man steals an ox or a sheep and slaughters it or sells it, he must pay back five head of cattle for the ox and four sheep for the sheep. A thief must certainly make restitution, but if he has nothing, he must be sold to pay for his theft."*[125]

Now that I abide in a place of restoration, healing and deliverance, I have a holy vengeance against the devil. What do I mean by that? In Luke 18:3, we see the parable of the persistent widow. It says, *"And there was a widow in that city who kept coming to him and saying, 'Give me justice against my adversary.'"*[126] She begged the judge for justice and restitution for what was taken from her. She was without a husband, without protection, and he was her only advocate.

The enemy came into my life and took life, peace, joy, sound mind, purity, friendship, and a family that were rightfully mine as a child of God. I am asking God to render a just verdict for me against my adversary. I have a fire inside me for not only restoration for me, but for restitution. The devil will have to pay back double for what he stole from me.

I not only want to have restitution for me but for all God's people who have been robbed of what's theirs. I want to see God's people come out of sexual, emotional, and alcoholic bondage. I want to see hope and healing restored to those who have been tormented by the devil so they can come out of the darkness and into the light of Jesus Christ. It is a burning passion in my heart to see God's people living in the fullness of what God has called them to be while living in freedom.

What has the devil stolen from you? Is it your child, your innocence, your health, your spouse? I want to lift both you and your loved one up in prayer:

"Father God, I pray that you would move swiftly on the behalf of these precious people who have experienced tremendous loss in their lives. Holy Spirit, I pray that you would ignite their heart with the fire of your love. Let them burn for you, and only you. You have the words of everlasting life and can restore all that was lost. In you, we find these things that were lost or stolen.

Father, Restore and give restitution for your people for all the years that were stolen from them. Give them back a double portion. What the enemy meant for evil, turn it around for their good. Restore all that was lost and bring your people back into your fold.

Release your Spirit now, and please move swiftly in the areas of discouragement and hopelessness. You make all things new. I release hope, restoration and restitution for each one. May it be done according to your Word, Amen.

Tenacious Faith

"Never, Never, Never, Never, Never Give Up." -Winston Churchill

I am a fan of UFC (Ultimate Fight Championship ®) fighting or MMA (Mixed Martial Arts) fighting. Some people don't care for it, but I like it. God often speaks to me through watching UFC® Fights. The first lesson God taught me through this was if I am going to get in the ring and face my opponent, I must know my strengths and weaknesses. When it pertains to your loved one, a weakness could be incorrectly directing your anger or giving up on God's goodness and promises. Strengths could be knowing He equips you for the battle, you're not fighting alone because God is with you, fighting for you, and your loved one.

The second was that it is vital to know my opponent's strategy for winning before the fight. If I'm not readily familiar with my opponent's strategy, I am easily susceptible to it. If you are going to fight for what is rightfully yours, you must come toe to toe with your opponent and be tenacious.

Tenacious means stubborn, relentless, unshakable, determined, strong-willed, and unwavering. Tenacity or stubbornness, in the hands of God, can be used for good, but stubbornness used for rebellion against God is dangerous. I know. I lived it.

You need to know what is rightfully yours before you can take any ground or authority over it. As believers, we have to stand and believe for what is rightfully ours. The persistent widow demonstrated how our determination can render justice. This tenacious faith is what moves Jesus' heart like no other. It also moves our heart to a deeper level of faith.

A great example of tenacity is the movie *Unbroken*. It is based on the true story of Olympian, Louis Zamperini, who fought for his life after being captured as a prisoner of war in Japan during WWII. His spirit could not be broken despite being tested by fire in every way imaginable. Louis would not give up even after being starved and beaten by a sadistic guard in the Japanese camp. Louis' tenacious spirit reflected that of sold-out Christ-follower, as he was forced to stand against the power of his mortal enemy.

As Christians, we are called to this kind of fight and unbroken spirit. After all, we have the same power that raised Jesus from the grave living inside of us. We have what it takes inside to live a life of tenacity. You may be beaten or bruised, and feel like there is nothing left in you to fight for your child, but I am telling you that's when God helps you rise up and go to another level of faith in Him.

God is alive in you, and you are called to be a warrior in His kingdom, to stand up and fight with a tenacious faith. Zechariah 4:6 says, *"Not by might, nor by power, but by my Spirit says the Lord Almighty."*[127] It's not enough to muster up faith in our own strength. We have to allow the Spirit of God to rise up and lead the way.

This is the time where we must have tenacity when we are believing and praying for this kind of revelation and transformation to take place. We must be intentional about it every day. We must press in and push through our feelings and believe just like the persistent widow. She was determined to get justice for what she knew was rightfully hers. She didn't back down because he said, "No" over and over again. She saw it as a delayed response. She didn't take no for an answer and neither should you.

Keep contending for your child! Never, never, never give up, no matter what! There is hope for freedom. I am living proof and an answer to my parent's tenacious prayers. My parents contended for me for years and never gave up on God's promises over my life.

I invite you to pray with me:

Father, release a spirit of tenacity for the restoration of their loved ones upon your people. Move their hearts to rise in faith like they never have before. Take them to a place of unwavering faith in you. I release the same power that Jesus Christ had at resurrection over them. I pray you will give them a warrior spirit that never settles for compromise and that never gives up. In Jesus' name, I release your anointing and the fullness of your glory upon them. Arise in Him and be ignited with tenacious faith!

About the Author

As a child, Dana always believed she would make a difference in this world. At the age of nineteen, Dana met  the love of her life, Jesus. His love was always calling her to something greater than herself.

Through a string of misunderstandings as a child, traumatic events, and personal decisions, Dana found herself in the throws of alcohol and emotional addictions and the lesbian lifestyle.

She felt trapped in an abyss that she couldn't escape on her own. God's relentless pursuit, through her many ups and downs of addiction and relationships, inspired her to share her story with you.

WWW.DANAEPPERLY.COM

WWW.RAISINGTHEWHITEFLAG.COM

WWW.HOPEFORFREEDOM.NET

WANT TO WORK WITH DANA?

Dana has a passion to share about experiencing freedom in Christ. She offers her services in several capacities like:

• Mentoring

• Speaking Engagements

• Life Coaching

• Youth Retreats

• Mission Trips

To check her availability for your next conference or event, go to WWW.DANAEPPERLY.COM.

WORKS CITED

All Scripture was cited from BibleGateway.com. The specific translation of each verse is noted in the end associated with that verse.

BibleGateway.com: A searchable online Bible in over 150 versions and 50 languages. May 03, 2016 through May 03, 2017, https://www.biblegateway.com.

1 The Judds, Curb Records, 2008.CD.

2 McGraw, Tim, and Faith Hill. "It's Your Love, with Faith Hill." Curb, 1996. CD.

3 NIV

4 Redman, Matt. Your Grace Finds Me. N.d. CD.

5 Daigle, Lauren. How Can it Be. N.d. CD.

6 NAB

7 NASB

8 NIV

9 Purkey, Mike. *Reverse the Devil's Decision*. Lake Mary, FL: Creation House, 2000. Print.

10 Scott, David. *The Love That Made Mother Teresa: How Her Secret Visions and Dark Nights Can Help You Conquer the Slums of Your Heart*. Manchester, NH: Sophia Institute Press, 2016. Print.

11 Moltmann, Jürgen. *The Crucified God*. London: SCM Press, 2015. Print.

12 KJV

13 NIV

14 Job 1:12

15 Job 19:1-12

16 NIV, Job 2:9-10

17 NIV

18 NAB

19 Purkey, Mike. *Reverse the Devil's Decision*. Lake Mary, FL: Creation House, 2000. Print.

20 NIV, John 10:10

21 NIV

22 NIV, Matt.17:20

23 KJV

24 Tutu, Desmond. www.brainyquote.com/quotes/d/desmond tut 454129.html. Retrieved 4/5/17.

25 NIV

26 NIV

27 NIV,

28 Purkey, Mike. Reverse the Devil's Decision. Lake Mary, FL: Creation House, 2000. Print.

29 NIV

30 KJV,

31 ESV,

32 NIV, John 8:36

33 KJV,

34 KJV,

35 NIV,

36 NIV,

37 ESV,

38 Meyer, Joyce. *Battlefield of the Mind: Winning the Battle in Your Mind*.: FAITHWORDS, 2017. Print.

39 NIV

40 NIV

41 Meyer, Joyce. meyer.org/Everydayanswers/teachings Retrieved 4/5/16.

42 NIV

43 NIV

44 ESV

45 NLT

46 NIV

47 NIV

48 Bowen, Trevor. www.insearchoftruth.org/articles/sin_of_presumption.html . Retrieved 4/5/17.

49 NAB

50 NIV

51 NIV

52 NIV

53 NIV,

54 NIV, Luke 15:11-32

55 NIV, Jude 1:19

56 NLT

57 Rowe, Anissa. https://m.facebook.com/defiancetrinity/posts/1111371282255480. Retrieved 4/5/17.

58 NAB

59 NAB

60 NAS

61 NIV

62 NET

63 NIV

64 NIV

65 Sorge, Bob. The Chastening of the Lord: The Forgotten Doctrine. Copyright 2016 by Bob Sorge. Published by Oasis House. PO Box 522 Grandview, Mo 64030 Pg.70.

66 NIV

67 NAS

68 St Joseph's Edition of the New American Bible. Copyright 1992, 1987, 1980, 1970 by Catholic Book Publishing Co. New York, N.Y. United States. (Page 1042).

69 St Joseph's Edition of the New American Bible. Copyright 1992, 1987, 1980, 1970 by Catholic Book Publishing Co. New York, N.Y. United States. (Page 1042).

70 ESV

71 NLT

72 Warren, Richard. *The Purpose-Driven Life: What on Earth am I Here For?* Grand Rapids, MI: Zondervan, 2016.Print.

73 Cioch, Bernadette. *Embracing the Wounds of Post-Traumatic Stress Disorder: An Invitation to Heal.* Totowa, NJ: Resurrection Press/ Catholic Book Pub., 2008. Print.

74 NIV, 2 Corinthians 12:7

75 Wikipedia. https://en.m.wikipedia.org/wiki/Kintsugi. Retrieved 4/5/17).

76 Lucado, Max. Max Lacado www.faithgateway.com/what-was-meant-for-evil-god-uses-for-good/#.WOVna6NOnJs. Retrieved 4/5/17.

77 Lucado, Max. Max Lacado www.faithgateway.com/what-was-meant-for-evil-god-uses-for-good/#.WOVna6NOnJs. Retrieved 4/5/17.

78 NIV

79 NLT

80 Lucado, Max. Max Lacado www.faithgateway.com/what-was-meant-for-evil-god-uses-for-good/#.WOVna6NOnJs. Retrieved 4/5/17.

81 Butler Brian, Jason Evert, and Crystalina Evert. *Theology of the Body for Teens: Discovering God's Plan for Love and Life: student workbook.* West Chester, PA: Ascension Press, 2006. Print. Page 13.

82 Butler Brian, Jason Evert, and Crystalina Evert. *Theology of the Body for Teens: Discovering God's Plan for Love and Life: student workbook.* West Chester, PA: Ascension Press, 2006. Print. Page 14.

83 NKJV

84 Paul, Pope John Paul II. Second Vatican Council. http://w2.vatican.va/content/john-paul-ii/en/encyclicals/documents/hf jp-ii enc 04031979 redemptor-hominis.html. Retrieved 4/2/17.

85 Healy, Mary. Scripture, Mercy, and Homosexuality. El Cajon, California: Catholic Answers, 2016. Print. (Page 72-73).

86 John 10:10

87 Genesis 1:31

88 Butler Brian, Jason Evert, and Crystalina Evert. *Theology of the Body for Teens: Discovering God's Plan for Love and Life: student workbook.* West Chester, PA: Ascension Press, 2006. Print.

89 Butler Brian, Jason Evert, and Crystalina Evert. *Theology of the Body for Teens: Discovering God's Plan for Love and Life: student workbook.* West Chester, PA: Ascension Press, 2006. Print. Page 42.

90 Paul, Pope John Paul II. 15th World Youth Day. Address of The Holy Father John Paul II www.goodreads.com/quotes/8031-it-is-jesus-that-you-seek-when-you-dream-of. Retrieved 4/5/17.

91 Butler Brian, Jason Evert, and Crystalina Evert. *Theology of the Body for Teens: Discovering God's Plan for Love and Life: student workbook.* West Chester, PA: Ascension Press, 2006. Print. Page 42.

92 KJV

93 Butler Brian, Jason Evert, and Crystalina Evert. *Theology of the Body for Teens: Discovering God's Plan for Love and Life: student workbook.* West Chester, PA: Ascension Press, 2006. Print. Page 42.

94 Butler Brian, Jason Evert, and Crystalina Evert. *Theology of the Body for Teens: Discovering God's Plan for Love and Life: student workbook.* West Chester, PA: Ascension Press, 2006. Print. Page 9.

95 Healy, Mary. Scripture, Mercy, and Homosexuality. El Cajon, California: Catholic Answers, 2016. Print. Page 22.

96 Healy, Mary. Scripture, Mercy, and Homosexuality. El Cajon, California: Catholic Answers, 2016. Print. Page 22.

97 Healy, Mary. Scripture, Mercy, and Homosexuality. El Cajon, California: Catholic Answers, 2016. Print. Page 22.

98 Healy, Mary. Scripture, Mercy, and Homosexuality. El Cajon, California: Catholic Answers, 2016. Print. Page 23.

99 Paul, Pope John Paul II. 15th World Youth Day. Address of The Holy Father John Paul II www.goodreads.com/quotes/8031-it-is-jesus-that-you-seek-when-you-dream-of. Retrieved 4/5/17.

100 NIV

101 KJV,

102 NLT

103 NAS

104 NIV

105 NAS, 1 Peter 1:15

106 KJV

107 NAS

108 St Joseph's Edition of the New American Bible. Copyright 1992, 1987, 1980, 1970 by Catholic Book Publishing Co. New York, N.Y. United States. Page 224.

109 ESV

110 ESV

111 Franklin, Lou. Desert Stream Ministries Newsletter 2016.

112 NET

113 ESV

114 ESV

[115] Comiskey, Andrew. Desert Stream Ministries Newsletter 2016.
[116] Comiskey, Andrew. Desert Stream Ministries Newsletter 2016
[117] NAS
[118] Hebrews 11:6
[119] NIV
[120] NIV
[121] KJV
[122] Purkey, Mike. Reverse the Devil's Decision. Lake Mary, FL. Creation House, 2000. Print.
[123] NIV
[124] NLT
[125] NET,
[126] ESV
[127] NIV

Made in the USA
Columbia, SC
10 June 2017